ONE-MINUTE ANSWERS

ANSWERS

to

Anti-Mormon QUESTIONS

ONE-MINUTE ANSWERS

to

Anti-Mormon QUESTIONS

Stephen W. Gibson

Fourth Printing: February, 2005

International Standard Book Number:

0-88290-784-0

Horizon Publishers' Catalog and Order Number:

C1060

Printed and distributed
in the United States of America by

Address:
925 North Main Street
Springville, Utah 84663

Local Phone: (801) 489-4084
Toll Free: 1 (800) SKYBOOK
FAX: (800) 489-1097

E-mail: skybook@cedarfort.com
Internet: http://www.cedarfort.com

Contents

Part 4
Answers to Questions About Church Doctrine

Part 5
Answers to Questions About Jesus Christ
and God the Father

Part 6
Questions and Answers
About Miscellaneous Items

Acknowledgments

I would like to express my deepest gratitude to the many people with whom I've worked to produce the ideas that are presented in this book, as well as for their support in helping me complete it.

My good friend and fellow Scottish missionary, Bill Forrest, together with our mutual friend, Van Hale, helped me in this project. They have been defenders of the faith for more than 20 years. They have co-authored many pamphlets, published under the *Mormon Miscellaneous* imprint, and have hosted hundreds of radio talk shows.

Malin Jacobs, Steve Mayfield, Kathy Taylor and numerous others helped me gather literature produced by critics of the LDS Church. Malin Jacobs also helped me with some of the weightier discussions I had years ago with the producers of the movie, *The God Makers.*

My family members, especially my oldest son, Stephen D. Gibson, gave me considerable help and encouragement. Stephen, fresh from the mission field, sequestered himself with Bill Forrest and me in a Colorado cabin for days. We searched the scriptures together and found Biblical parallels related to some of the most often-asked questions presented by our detractors.

My friend, BYU professor George Pace, reviewed the manuscript and made suggestions based on his decades of New Testament and gospel study. Finally, my friend Giles Florence and Horizon Publishers' editor Lorin May and Senior Editor Duane S. Crowther made many important suggestions and improvements in the book.

All these friends and helpers joined me in this project. I express my profound appreciation to them all for their invaluable assistance and encouragement.

Introduction

This book was written for you—an average member of the Church who may have come across an anti-Mormon tract somewhere along the way and have not taken the time to search out the answers to some of the questions posed in it.

Or, you may have casually browsed through an LDS book written to answer these questions hoping to find the answer, but you lost interest because of the frequency of scholarly terms used, or were put off by the large number of Greek, Aramaic, or Hebrew words. Or, perhaps there were a lot of statements from the early Christian Fathers, or names you didn't recognize or didn't have the time or interest to research.

You really didn't want to learn a new language or study early Christian history. You just wanted the question answered quickly and simply. I hope you will find in this book the answer to some question that has personally concerned you. *One-Minute Answers* was written to do just that.

This book contains concise, easy-to-understand answers to questions frequently found in anti-Mormon pamphlets today. I have read hundreds of these pamphlets and see many of the same questions over and over.

I have selected the 61 questions that I see most often and have provided quick, common-sense answers to them. Occasionally, because a few questions are more complex, some of my answers are longer or more detailed, but you won't find a discussion that takes a doctoral degree to understand, because I can't write that way.

Some who read the manuscript of this book felt a few of the questions were inane and didn't deserve a response. I, too, think a lot of the questions are absurd; however, I didn't make up the questions—anti-Mormons did. Therefore, answers to "silly" questions have also been included.

Please don't use these answers as ammunition to take on a local anti-Mormon. If I have learned anything over the years of talking with some of the most renowned opponents of the Church, it is that conversion does not come through argument or scripture bashing. It comes only through honest inquiry and prayerful consideration. Most of the anti-Mormons I have met refuse to do either.

Conversion comes in great part through the Spirit, not solely from the intellect. The intellect, however, can confirm what the Spirit has indicated. It is for that purpose that I have written this book—to aid the reader in understanding important concepts so that lack of knowledge on these points can cease to be an obstacle to spiritual growth.

Part 1

Answers to
Questions
About

The
Book
of
Mormon

14

Notes

1
Does It Quote Shakespeare?

Question: Didn't Joseph Smith quote from William Shakespeare in 2 Nephi 1:14?

While it is true that both the Book of Mormon and William Shakespeare used forms of the phrase "from which no traveler can return," critics are far from proving plagiarism. Let us look at the facts.

First, if one uses three words such as "Give me liberty," is he plagiarizing Patrick Henry, or did he just have similar thoughts? Obviously, a similarity of short phrases does not prove plagiarism.

Second, one would have to show that Joseph Smith not only had access to the works of Shakespeare (something which certainly has not been proven by those making the accusation), but that he actually read the Bard of Avon. This would be highly unlikely for an unlearned farmer boy.

Third, some scholars now claim that Shakespeare himself borrowed many phrases from the Bible as he wrote Hamlet, Act 3. This is particularly evident from reading the Geneva Bible version of Job 10:21. The very phrase that anti-Mormon critics accuse Joseph Smith of "borrowing from Shakespeare" is repeated at least six times in the Old Testament.

If this phrase was an inspired thought for Job, David, and other prophets in the Old Testament, it could certainly be an inspired thought from the same God to the prophet Lehi. Perhaps, then, Shakespeare himself "borrowed" it first from the Old Testament—

the same place from which Joseph Smith may have borrowed that wording. Or perhaps, as one researcher said, "Shakespeare may have received by theft what Joseph Smith received by inspiration."

FARMS researchers have shown that the idea and expression in 2 Nephi 1:13-15 was abundantly used from Mesopotamia to Egypt during Lehi's time. Joseph Smith had no way of knowing how commonly the thought "from which there is no return" was used anciently, but Lehi felt comfortable using it.

Finally, we have no right to limit the Lord. When someone says that God will not or cannot inspire different men in different places in different times with the same information or thoughts (i.e., Lehi, Job, Joseph Smith, and even Shakespeare), they are attempting to limit Jesus Christ and the Holy Ghost. This fallacy is certainly non-Biblical.

2
Why Is the French Word Adieu Used?

Question: How could Book of Mormon writer Jacob, who lived about 500 B.C., use the French word "adieu" (Jacob 7:27) when the French language wasn't even developed until A.D. 1500?

Those who ask this question must either forget that the Book of Mormon (and for that matter, the Bible) is a translation from another language, or perhaps they don't realize that a translator uses the words in his vocabulary which he feels will best portray the meaning of the original writer's or speaker's thoughts to current readers.

Strictly speaking, no words in the Book of Mormon are Jacob's words, or the words of any other prophet of that period. "Adieu" was probably the best equivalent of Jacob's words of which Joseph Smith was aware. So, whether it is "adieu" or "constraineth" or "abomination," they are modern translations of ancient words.

It is interesting to note that Daniel H. Ludlow, an LDS Church scholar, has found a Hebrew word that means the same or nearly the same as Adieu. It is "Lehitra'ot" (*A Companion to Your Study of the Book of Mormon*, p. 163). Both words mean "I commend you to God."

A Biblical parallel detractors should consider is the use of the word "compass" in the Old and New Testament. Most scholars credit Chinese navigators with the invention of the compass around A.D. 1000 (*World Book Encyclopedia*, Vol. 4, 1972, p. 735), which is nearly 1,000 years after the latest reference to a compass in Acts

28:13. Certainly this easily explained problem of word choices would not shake anyone's faith in the Bible. Nor should the word choice of a 19th-century prophet shake anyone's faith in the Book of Mormon.

Another example of an equivalent modern word in the Bible is the use of "Easter" in the King James version of Acts 12:4. Most modern translations reject this modern word in favor of the ancient term "Passover."

The author once asked a Church of Christ minister about the words *compass* and *Easter* in the Bible. His answer was, "Obviously there was a mistake in translation." Because of translation issues and errors, Joseph Smith wrote in our eighth Article of Faith: "We believe the Bible to be the word of God as far as it is translated correctly; we also believe the Book of Mormon to be the word of God."

3

Did It Give the Wrong Birthplace for Jesus?

Question: How can anyone believe the Book of Mormon when it doesn't even get the birthplace of Jesus Christ right?

This question refers to Alma 7:10, where Alma prophesied that Jesus Christ "shall be born of Mary, at [the land of] Jerusalem which is the land of our forefathers." It is noteworthy that Alma did not speak of Christ being born *in* the city of Jerusalem, but *at* Jerusalem. This is a significant difference.

There are at least two possible explanations for Alma 7:10. That offered by the critics is that no prophet named Alma wrote these words. They assume that Joseph Smith wrote the Book of Mormon, and at age 24, didn't know that Christ was born in Bethlehem. This idea is illogical considering that nearly everyone at the time of Joseph Smith understood that the Savior was born in Bethlehem. It is also inconsistent because Joseph Smith is recognized by even his most hated enemies as a person of unusual intellect.

The second explanation—accepted by most Latter-day Saints—is that in the year 82 B.C., Alma did live and taught that Christ "shall be born of Mary, at [the land of] Jerusalem which is the land of our forefathers" (Alma 7:10). Proof of the historical and linguistic accuracy of Alma's statement is found in the Armana letters, where it is recorded that in Palestine and Syria, a large area around a city and all the inhabitants of that area bore the name of the city.

Bethlehem is only five miles south of the much larger city of Jerusalem. Thus, a citizen of Bethlehem could have accurately described himself as a person who lived "at Jerusalem." Rather than Alma's comment being evidence of Joseph Smith's fraud, it is in reality a confirmation of his inspiration.

Today, the further we are away from our home or any specific town, the more likely we are to "lump it" with the closest large metropolitan area. If we are visiting New York we might tell people we are from Salt Lake City rather than Bluffdale, Utah. If we are in Europe we might tell someone that we are from Utah, or possibly we might say we are from the United States. When we say that, we aren't in error; we are just not being as specific as we could be.

A final thought: if Joseph Smith or later Church leaders felt this to be an error, why didn't they "correct" it and make it one of the many "wholesale" changes the detractors are always accusing the Church leaders of making in the Book of Mormon? Latter-day Saints find no contradiction with Christ being born "at Jerusalem," the land of the forefathers of Alma and his people.

Suggested reading:

Sperry, *Problems of the Book of Mormon,* pp. 131-36.
Nibley, *An Approach to the Book of Mormon,* pp. 80-82.

4
Does It Quote the King James Bible?

Question: *Doesn't the fact that the Book of Mormon quotes from the King James translation of the Bible, including the italicized words, prove that it is not a divinely inspired translation?*

Of the approximately 264 thousand words in the Book of Mormon, about 17 thousand are close parallels to the King James translation of the Bible. Most parallel verses occurred when Nephi quoted the Isaiah of the Old Testament using records on brass plates brought from Jerusalem. Other parallels occurred when the resurrected Savior repeated his Sermon on the Mount to the Nephites and then quoted Malachi at length. In both cases, we are told in the text that these are quotations of scriptures that had been recorded elsewhere.

Joseph Smith left no record of how he translated the plates beyond saying that it was done by the power of God. LDS scholars generally agree that in instances where the Book of Mormon parallels the Bible, Joseph Smith must have noted the parallels and used the King James Bible to guide him in his choice of words. If the Book of Mormon agreed with the Biblical text in meaning, he apparently utilized the Biblical text, italicized words and all. However, when the plates differed from the Biblical text, he followed the text on the plates.

For example, of 433 verses of Isaiah quoted in the Book of Mormon, 46 percent are identical to those in the Bible, while 54 percent are modified to some extent. These diffcrent verses have been of great use to LDS scholars. Several Hebrew literary structures are found only in a degraded form in the King James Bible, while those literary structures are complete and intact in the Book of Mormon. This shows that the brass plates version found in the Book of Mormon was a different, older Isaiah text.

A slightly more difficult problem is posed by Book of Mormon similarities with Biblical scriptures which were not in existence when Lehi left Jerusalem. For instance, Moroni 7:45, 46 parallels 1 Corinthians 13:4-8 (Paul's discussion on charity) so closely that some explanation is called for.

Mormon, Moroni's father, lived after Christ and knew Christ's teachings. Since the ultimate source of Paul's teachings was also Christ, it should not be surprising to find both Mormon and Paul teaching the same thing. The fact that both wrote on charity indicates the importance of this gospel concept.

If Mormon delivered a sermon on charity, it could logically contain much of the same material as Paul's teachings on the same subject. However, one would not expect identical, word-for-word renderings of the two writings, and indeed they are not totally identical. Two significant clauses found in 1 Corinthians are absent from Mormon's sermon, and Mormon's definition of charity is absent from Paul's writings. Nonetheless, several phrases are identical. These identical phrases are understood the same way as the Isaiah passages by Latter-day Saints: Joseph Smith recognized Mormon's teachings as similar to Paul's and likely used the biblical text where it agreed in meaning with the plates. Where the meanings differed, he followed the plates.

Since the ultimate source of the teachings of the Book of Mormon is Christ, and since the ultimate source of the teachings of the Bible (both Old and New Testaments) is also Christ, it should surprise no one that there are many parallels between Book of Mormon and Bible passages. While one cannot conclusively prove that Joseph Smith used a King James Bible as an aid in translating the parallel passages, that explanation is reasonable.

The reader is invited to consult the references listed below for a much more detailed discussion of this question.

Gorton, *Legacy of the Brass Plates of Laban.*
Nibley, *Since Cumorah,* pp. 123-52.
B. H. Roberts, "Bible Quotations in the Book of Mormon," *Improvement Era* 7, January, 1904, reprinted in *A Book of Mormon Treasury,* pp. 173-89.
Sperry, *The Problems of the Book of Mormon,* pp. 73-121, 206-07.

5
Does It Contradict the Bible?

Question: The Bible says that the followers of Christ were first called Christians in Antioch a few years after Christ died (Acts 11:26). The Book of Mormon says there were people called Christians in 73 BC. Doesn't the Book of Mormon contradict the Bible?

It doesn't take a lot of scholarship to show there is no contradiction in this situation. "Christian" wasn't the original word used in either the Biblical text or on the plates in the Book of Alma. "Christian" is an English word, and neither the Bible nor the Book of Mormon was originally written in English:

Even if both sources had used the very same word, the fact that Luke wrote that the word "Christian" was first used in Antioch would be proof of nothing. He had no knowledge that a prophet in the New World had used a similar term to label the followers of Christ one hundred years earlier.

The word "Christians" is the word Joseph Smith chose to use while translating Alma 46:13-15. Apparently it was the word in his vocabulary that came closest to the word originally used on the plates.

6
Does the Doctrine and Covenants Contradict It?

Question: The Book of Mormon states that the many wives and concubines of David and Solomon were an abomination before the Lord (Jacob 2:23-24). But Doctrine and Covenants 132:38 contradicts the Book of Mormon and says David and Solomon didn't sin. Is this a contradiction in the Standard Works?

David, as a polygamist, did that which was right in the eyes of the Lord until he took the wife of Uriah, according to both the Bible and the Doctrine and Covenants. The Bible says,

> Because David did that which was right in the eyes of the Lord, and turned not aside from any thing that he commanded him all the days of his life, save only in the matter of Uriah the Hittite (1 Kings 15:5).

The Bible tells us that David's wives were given to him by the Lord through his prophet, Nathan, who is also mentioned in Doctrine and Covenants 132:39. David, however, sinned greatly in the case of Uriah, so much that the scriptures tell us he has fallen from his exaltation (D & C 132:39).

In the case of Solomon (1 Kings 11:1-6), his situation was truly an abomination because he took unauthorized, non-Israelite, pagan wives and concubines. The result was that his wives turned his heart against God and toward pagan gods, in spite of the fact that God had appeared to Solomon twice:

But King Solomon loved many strange women, together with the daughter of Pharaoh, women of the Moabites, Ammonites, Edomites, Zidonians, and Hittites;

Of the nations concerning which the Lord said unto the children of Israel, Ye shall not go in to them, neither shall they come in unto you: for surely they will turn away your heart after their gods; Solomon clave unto these in love.

And he had seven hundred wives, princesses, and three hundred concubines; and his wives turned away his heart.

For it came to pass, when Solomon was old, that his wives turned away his heart after other gods; and his heart was not perfect with the Lord his God, as was the heart of David, his father.

For Solomon went after Ashtoreth the goddess of the Zidonians, and after Milcom the abomination of the Ammonites.

And Solomon did evil in the sight of the Lord, and went not fully after the Lord, as did David his father (1 Kings. 11:1-6).

The Doctrine and Covenants agrees with the Bible. The Lord, in speaking to Jacob in the Book of Mormon, knew the minds of the people and that they were excusing their own sins by comparing themselves to David and Solomon. Why, out of all the Biblical kings and prophets who were polygamists, were David and Solomon singled out for criticism by the Lord? Because they sinned in the taking of unlawful wives, i.e., David in the case of Bathsheba (1 Kings 15:5) and Solomon with his foreign wives.

This "thing," the taking of *unauthorized* wives, was the sin and abomination Jacob warned of, *not* the marrying of additional wives given by the Lord's prophets.

7
Why is Christ Only "A" Son of God?

Question: How can Latter-day Saints be Christians when the Book of Mormon states that Christ is just "a" son of God, not "the" son of God (Alma 36:17)?

One can be amazed at how many truths one overlooked in their search to find one point which anti-Mormon writers can claim to be an error or a fault. The Book of Mormon refers to Christ as *the* son of God at least 50 times and refers to him as *a son* of God only once. To conclude from that single example that we think less of him because Alma referred to him as *a son* rather than *the son* is not only foolish but hypocritical. It certainly is an example of what length critics will go to as they try to find new things to trip up LDS members.

In the Bible, we find a parallel in Luke 2:11: "For unto you is born this day in the city of David *a Saviour,* which is Christ the Lord." Using the same logic as the critics, could we then say someone who believes in Luke 2:11 is not a Christian since he believes Christ is just *a Savior,* not *the Savior?* Of course not. Another example from the Bible referring to Christ as *a son* is found in Hebrews 5:8, "Though he were *a Son,* yet learned he obedience by the things which he suffered."

In Latter-day Saint theology, Christ is both *a son* of God and *the son* of God. He is *a Savior* and *the Savior,* but most importantly he is *our* personal Savior. He died for each of us.

The major difference between his sonship and that of other off-spring of Heavenly Father is that Jesus Christ is the "only begotten Son" (that is, in the flesh) (John 3:16). Perhaps even greater evidence of the centrality of Christ in the Restored Church is the fact that the 531 pages of the Book of Mormon contain 3,925 references to the Savior. That is one reference every one and one-half verses!

8
Was It Based On
View of the Hebrews?

Question: Didn't Joseph Smith get some of his ideas for the Book of Mormon from reading View of the Hebrews, *which was first published in 1823, seven years before the Book of Mormon was published?*

The two books, *View of the Hebrews* and *The Book of Mormon* have been undergoing comparisons for decades. When B. H. Roberts did his work on the two in 1922, interest in the parallels grew. In addition, Fawn Brodie's book, *No Man Knows My History,* and G. T. Harrison's fictitious book, *Mormons are Peculiar People,* raised public awareness about some similarities between the two books.

View of the Hebrews is one of perhaps half a dozen pre-1830 books supporting the thesis that the American Indians (or Native Americans) were of Hebrew origin. It was written by a minister who lived in Vermont, on the other end of the state from where Joseph Smith was born.

There is no evidence that Joseph Smith ever knew Ethan Smith or ever read *View of the Hebrews* prior to the publication of the Book of Mormon. Fawn Brodie admits such herself. However, after so stating, she continues to write as if Joseph Smith had access to the book as he was "writing" the Book of Mormon. *View of the Hebrews* is Ethan Smith's compilation of what writers, explorers, and some who were raised by Indians observed about Indian traditions and their own stories of their origins. Ethan Smith selected and arranged these quotes to support his thesis that the Indians were descendants of the Lost Ten Tribes of Israel and that they came to the New World by crossing the Bering Strait.

B. H. Robert's conclusions were that *if* Joseph Smith had *written* the Book of Mormon himself, he certainly could have gotten some of his ideas from *View of the Hebrews*. The author agrees with that conclusion. However, B. H. Roberts had strong faith in the divine origin of the Book of Mormon, a fact to which he testified many times after he made his 1922 comparison of the two books.

The author personally doubts that even if Joseph Smith had a copy of *View of the Hebrews* prior to his translating the Book of Mormon, he would have ploughed through the first 150 pages of the book necessary to get to any of the parallels.

Let us now examine the books and note some of their parallels and some of their differences:

View of the Hebrews has ten tribes leaving Jerusalem around 763 BC and traveling across the Bering Strait with God drying out the earth so they could walk across it, a journey that took one-and-a-half years. The Book of Mormon shows the families of Lehi and Ishmael (members of two tribes) wandering in the wilderness for eight years before boarding a boat built by Nephi and crossing the Pacific Ocean.

Noticeably missing in *View of the Hebrews,* but very apparent in the Book of Mormon, is constant communication between God and his people through holy prophets. The ten tribes, according to the traditions recorded by Ethan Smith, had a holy book but it was taken from them before they arrived in the Americas from Jerusalem. The Book of Mormon people experienced just the opposite. They obtained a holy book just prior to leaving Jerusalem and brought it with them to the Americas.

View of the Hebrews develops a strong case for Hebrew traditions that were evident, according to those telling the story, among the Indians. These practices include circumcision, Indian imitation of the Ark of the Covenant made by carrying a small square box on their backs, the building of temples, a great high priest, life regulated by the number seven (moons, years, etc.), cities of refuge, years of Jubilee, not eating blood of their game and numerous other

Hebrew traditions. Of the above-mentioned items, only the building of temples is mentioned in the Book of Mormon.

The Book of Mormon, on the other hand, gives little detail about Mosaic rituals, yet contains numerous details of Christian rituals such as baptism. It also describes the understanding of redemption and the plan of salvation held among those who lived before Christ.

Both books tell of a more civilized segment of the people who were, through a series of wars, almost killed off while their more savage brothers continued to dominate. *View of the Hebrews* people migrated South from the Bering Strait, while Book of Mormon people generally moved northward from their original land. *View of the Hebrews* people had neither books nor the ability to write, and they became savages; Book of Mormon people were great record keepers, had prophets, and enjoyed a highly developed civilization.

Found among both books were temples and frequent references to Isaiah. However, in the Book of Mormon, it is the prophets among the people who have a great love for Isaiah. In *View of the Hebrews,* it is Ethan Smith who quotes freely from Isaiah, although generally from different chapters than those quoted in the Book of Mormon.

There are so many spiritually enlightening and motivating passages and details in the Book of Mormon about salvation, the atonement and Jesus Christ himself that it makes *View of the Hebrews* pale by comparison.

Before one seriously adopts the position that the Book of Mormon was hatched from *View of the Hebrews,* one must carefully read both. The author believes one will find *View of the Hebrews,* as with many books about the origin of the Native Americans, to be supportive of the Book of Mormon.

If a book showing parallels between Hebrew and Native American cultures was written after the Book of Mormon, detractors pay no attention to it. If written before, many try to prove that Joseph Smith somehow had access to it and used it as a source document for the Book of Mormon.

Having carefully read both, the author clearly finds parallels between the two books to be the exception rather than the rule.

For further reading on the similarities and differences of the two books, consult:

The Truth about "The God Makers," pp. 164-68.
Joseph Smith and the Beginnings of Mormonism, pp. 135-39.
"The Case of the Missing Phylactery," American Antiquarian Society.
Truman Madsen, "B. H. Roberts, and the Book of Mormon," BYU Studies, Summer 1979, p. 441.
"View of the Hebrews: An Unparallel," FARMS.

9
Where Is Its
"Fulness of the Gospel?"

Question: The Book of Mormon is supposed to contain the "Fulness of the gospel" (D & C 20:9), yet it mentions nothing about temple marriage, sealing ordinances, or baptism for the dead. According to Mormon theology, aren't these part of the fulness of the gospel?

This argument rests on the erroneous premise that "fulness" means every point of doctrine relating to every conceivable gospel topic. Obviously no one book of scripture, or even all the Standard Works together, contain "every conceivable doctrine." In fact, the scriptures are clear that God will yet reveal many great truths (Amos 3:7, John 16:12).

The Book of Mormon gives us a clear understanding of what is needed to truly follow the example of Christ and be "saved" in the Kingdom of God (3 Nephi 11:33). It is required that we have faith in Christ, repent of our sins, be baptized with water and the Holy Ghost and endure in righteousness to the end (see all of 2 Nephi 31 and 32). One might add that the fulness of the gospel, in addition to the above, embraces the atonement of Christ and the universal judgment. (3 Nephi 27:13-21).

As to the higher ordinances necessary for exaltation (after one enjoys the companionship of the Holy Ghost), it is probably of those ordinances the Lord was speaking when he said, "If thou shalt ask, thou shalt receive revelation upon revelation, knowledge upon knowledge, that thou mayest know the mysteries and peaceable things—that which bringeth joy, that which bringeth life eternal" (D & C 42:61).

As Latter-day Saints, we have the promise that a time is coming when this fulness will be preached to all:

> For it shall come to pass in that day, that every man shall hear the fulness of the gospel in his own tongue, and in his own language, through those who are ordained unto this power, by the administration of the Comforter, shed forth upon them for the revelation of Jesus Christ (D & C 90:11).

The fulness of the gospel that will be taught to all is the "doctrine of Christ." See also 3 Nephi 11:28-40; D & C 10:67.

10
Does It Forbid Polygamy?

Question: How can Latter-day Saints claim to follow the Book of Mormon when it specifically forbids having more than one wife?

This criticism is a fine example of taking something out of context, or of not reading an entire passage. Let us quote Jacob 2:27-29:

> Wherefore, my brethren, hear me, and hearken to the word of the Lord: For there shall not any man have save it be one wife; and concubines he shall have none;
> For I, the Lord God, delight in the chastity of women. And whoredoms are an abomination before me; thus saith the Lord of Hosts.
> Wherefore, this people shall keep my commandments, saith the Lord of Hosts, or cursed be the land for their sakes.

Seems obvious doesn't it? The Nephites weren't to have more than one wife. There is only one exception, however, to this rule. To understand it, we need to read one more verse—verse 30:

> For if I will, saith the Lord of Hosts, raise up seed unto me, I will command my people; otherwise they shall hearken unto these things.

The one exception would be if the Lord commands his people to live otherwise—to raise up a righteous seed—as he did in Old Testament times as well as in the early days of the Restored Church.

Today we continue to live as we have been commanded by the Lord through His prophets; that is, with one wife for each man.

It is interesting that nowhere in the Bible is there wholesale condemnation of the practice of plural marriage. In fact, many of the great men venerated by Christianity had more than one wife: David, Solomon, Abraham, Isaac, Jacob, and many others. As we attempt to understand the doctrine of plural marriage, perhaps it would be helpful to remember that the Lord sent his Only Begotten Son through polygamous lines (Abraham, Isaac, and Jacob). Surely that fact alone indicates the Lord's approval of this practice when he commands it.

The God of Abraham, Isaac and Jacob is a God who upon occasion gives more than one wife to a righteous man. Obviously, God has different rules and policies for different times. Plural marriage is righteous and acceptable conduct if God commands it through his prophet, but it is an abomination when the Lord has not commanded it.

11
Did the Smithsonian Refute It?

Question: If the Book of Mormon is true, why does the Smithsonian Institute put out letters stating that there is no connection between the Book of Mormon and Central and South American archaeology?

Archæological evidence or the lack thereof in no way affects the truthfulness of the Book of Mormon. If someone's testimony of the Book of Mormon is dependent on archæological digs, that person had better get a more profound spiritual confirmation.

Actually, the Smithsonian Institute is not giving support to anti-Mormons. The intent of their letter obviously is to back out of the debate, not to support one side's position. Their standard letter simply states that the Smithsonian staff knows of no supporting archæological evidence for the truthfulness of the book. While the standard letter has varied over the years, John L. Sorenson has evaluated the 1979 version of the letter from the Institute. He has made the following points:

1. The Smithsonian institute claims to have no staff members that are qualified to speak about the Book of Mormon.

2. While the Smithsonian scientists are qualified to discuss archæology, they do not claim to know everything there is to know about New World archæology.

3. Equally well-qualified, non-Smithsonian (and also non-Mormon) scientists have sharply disagreed with the Smithsonian

scientists on questions which are pertinent to Book of Mormon archæology and anthropology.

4. At least one of the form-letter's statements about New World archæology, one which detractors use against the Book of Mormon, has been contradicted by one of the Smithsonian's own scientists.

5. Several of the materials that the Smithsonian letter says were not used in pre-Columbian America were, in fact, in use by the Indians of Mexico, according to reports by the first Spaniards to come to the American continent.

In Joseph Smith's day there was no archæological evidence for many cultural items mentioned in the Book of Mormon, but in the last 30 to 50 years evidence has been found for those items. At the time the Book of Mormon was published, and for up to 100 years afterwards, scholars scoffed at the mention of glass, iron, and steel dating back two thousand years before Christ. However, archæologists, anthropologists, and other scientists no longer argue the credibility of such claims in the Book of Mormon as more and more significant evidence comes to light.

For example, the December, 1983 issue of *Science 83* magazine announced the discovery of pre-Columbian barley in the New World. This is one more example of items mentioned in the Book of Mormon, the pre-Columbian use of which was unknown in Joseph Smith's day.

While archæology can establish the existence of a civilization, the lack of archæological evidence doesn't prove a civilization didn't exist. In 1975, the civilization of Ebla was discovered, though prior to this time no one could produce an artifact associated with the Ebla people. It is examples like these which demonstrate the utter nonsense of statements such as, "Archæology has proved the existence of all great civilizations" (*The Godmakers* film).

Archæologists in the Americas and around the world continually find evidence that they cannot piece together into a conclusive picture. Evidence collected in the Americas is likewise too scattered to either prove or disprove that Nephites once lived on this continent or that the American Indians were once called Lamanites.

It would be interesting if the Smithsonian wrote a letter regarding archæological proof of the Bible.

For additional information see:

Nibley, *Since Cumorah.* (1967).
Nibley, *Lehi in the Desert and the World of the Jaredites.*
Sorenson, "An Evaluation of the Smithsonian Institution's Statement Regarding the Book of Mormon," Preliminary Report, Foundation for Ancient Research & Mormon Studies.

12
Why Were 4,000 Changes Made?

Question: If the LDS Church really believes the Book of Mormon is the word of God and, as Joseph Smith said, "the most perfect of any book on earth," why have there been more than 4,000 changes in it?

As is evident from his statement, Joseph Smith was referring to the book's precepts—the doctrines it contains which bring a man to God. First of all, anti-Mormon detractors often misquote Joseph Smith, and they have done so on this statement. Joseph Smith never said it was a perfect book. What he said, in a meeting with the Twelve on November 28, 1841, is recorded in *History of the Church,* Vol. 4, p. 461, as follows, "I told the brethren that the Book of Mormon was the most correct of any book on earth, and the keystone of our religion, and a man would get nearer to God by abiding by its precepts, than by any other book." Joseph's statement does not mean correct as far as spelling, grammar, or punctuation, but correct as to its historical origin and doctrinal precepts.

Anti-Mormon criticisms of changes in the Book of Mormon have their roots in Evangelical beliefs pertaining to what they regard as the "inerrancy of the Bible." Yet to sustain their belief in the Bible's inerrancy, in the light of the many thousands of changes and variations which exist in the numerous manuscripts and translations, they typically hedge their definitions of inerrancy with numerous limitations such as the following which are summarized from *The Moody Handbook of Theology,* pp. 166-70:

1. inerrancy is limited to the original manuscripts,
2. inerrancy allows for variety in style,
3. inerrancy allows for variety in details in explaining the same event,
4. inerrancy does not demand verbatim reporting of events,
5. inerrancy allows for departure from standard forms of grammar,
6. inerrancy allows for problem passages, and
7. inerrancy demands the account does not teach error or contradiction.

The anti-Mormon detractors who criticize the changes made in the Book of Mormon are seeking to impose a different standard on the Mormon scripture than they claim for the Bible. If the criteria listed above are applied to the Book of Mormon, then their criticism is completely lacking in merit and is valueless.

While it is true that there have been several thousand of changes made in the Book of Mormon since its first printing, the vast majority, have been punctuation, spelling and minor grammatical corrections. However, there have been other changes in addition to these.

As Joseph Smith made the translation from the plates, Oliver Cowdery, as well as other scribes, wrote down Joseph Smith's words as they heard them. Some errors occurred there, such as the substitution of the word "straight" for "strait."

The first manuscript written by the scribes was called "the original manuscript." Oliver Cowdery, in preparation for printing, hand copied the original manuscript to make a printer's copy, which was delivered several pages at a time to the printing firm of E. B. Grandin. In the copying, Oliver made additional errors.

The following statement by John H. Gilbert, the typesetter who worked for Grandin, sheds considerable light on the need for later changes. From his account (which was written on September 8, 1892, when he was 93 years old), we learn that he was twenty-seven in August, 1829 when the seven-month project of typesetting and printing the Book of Mormon was begun. From his memorandum it is apparent that he definitely was not a highly skilled grammarian. He wrote:

In the forepart of June 1829, Mr. E. B. Grandin, the printer of the "Wayne Sentinel," came to me and said he wanted I should assist him in estimating the cost of printing 5000 copies of a book that Martin Harris wanted to get printed, which he called the "Mormon Bible."

It was the second application of Harris to Grandin to do the job,—Harris assuring Grandin that the book would be printed in Rochester if he declined the job again.

Harris proposed to have Grandin do the job, if he would, as it would be quite expensive to keep a man in Rochester during the printing of the book, who would have to visit Palmyra two or three times a week for manuscript, &c. Mr. Grandin consented to do the job if his terms were accepted.

A few pages of the manuscript were submitted as a specimen of the whole, and it was said there would be about 500 pages.

The size of the page was agreed upon, and an estimate of the number of ems in a page, which would be 1000, and that a page of manuscript would make more than a page of printed matter, which proved to be correct.

The contract was to print and bind with leather, 5000 copies for $3,000. Mr. Grandin got a new font of Small Pica, on which the body of the work was printed. When the printer was ready to commence work, Harris was notified, and Hyrum Smith brought the first installment of manuscript, of 24 pages, closely written on common foolscap paper—he had it under his vest, and vest and coat closely buttoned over it. At night Smith came and got the manuscript, and with the same precaution carried it away. The next morning with the same watchfulness, he brought it again, and at night took it away. This was kept up for several days. The title page was first set up, and after proof was read and corrected, several copies were printed for Harris and his friends. On the second day—Harris and Smith being in the office—I called their attention to a grammatical error, and asked whether I should correct it? Harris consulted with Smith a short time, and turned to me and said: "The Old Testament is ungrammatical, set it as it is written."

After working a few days, I said to Smith on his handing me the manuscript in the morning; "Mr. Smith, if you would leave this manuscript with me, I would take it home with me at night and read and punctuate it." His reply was, "We are commanded not to leave it." A few mornings after this, when Smith handed me this manuscript, he said to me, "If you will give me your word that this manuscript shall be returned to us when you get through with it, I will leave it with you." I assured Smith that it should be returned all right when I got through with it. For two or three nights I took it home with me and read it, and punctuated it with a lead pencil. (This will account for the punctuation marks in pencil, which is referred to in the Mormon Report, an extract from which will be found below).

Martin Harris, Hyrum Smith and Oliver Cowdery were very frequent visitors to the office during the printing of the Mormon Bible. The manuscript was supposed to be in the handwriting of Cowdery. *Every Chapter, if I remember correctly, was one solid paragraph, without a punctuation mark, from beginning to end.*

Names of persons and places were generally capitalized, but *sentences had no end.* The character or short &, was used almost invariably where the word and, occurred, except at the end of a chapter. *I punctuated it to make it read as I supposed the Author intended, and but very little punctuation was altered in proofreading.* The Bible was printed 16 pages at a time, so that one sheet of paper made two copies of 16 pages each, requiring 2500 sheets of paper for each form of 16 pages. There were 37 forms of 16 pages each,—570 pages in all.

The work was commenced in August 1829, and finished in March 1830, seven months. Mr. J. H. Bortles and myself done the press work until December taking nearly three days to each form, . . .

Cowdery held and looked over the manuscript when most of the proofs were read. Martin Harris once or twice, and Hyrum Smith once, Grandin supposing these men could read their own writing as well, if not better, than anyone else; and if there are any discrepancies between the Palmyra edition and the manuscript these men should be held responsible.

Joseph Smith, Jr. had nothing to do whatever with the printing or furnishing copy for the printers, being but once in the office during the printing of the Bible, and then not over 15 or 20 minutes. (Wilford C. Wood, *Joseph Smith Begins His Work,* Vol. 1, pp. 30-31 [unnumbered]).

It is obvious that the first edition of the Book of Mormon was punctuated and then typeset (by hand, one letter at a time) by a young, relatively unskilled worker and was proofread by completely inexperienced proofreaders.

As he reviewed the printed First Edition, the Prophet Joseph Smith made more than a thousand alterations before the second edition was printed in 1837. These included typographical, spelling, and grammatical corrections as well as the addition of some minor clarifications. As late as 15 January 1842 (less than two years before his martyrdom), Joseph Smith was still making corrections. The first European edition published in 1841 used the 1837 edition as its basis, thereby perpetuating errors that had already been corrected in the 1840 American edition.

Three major editions have been published since, under the direction of either the President of the Church or the First Presidency. President John Taylor asked Orson Pratt to prepare the 1879 edition, which included such changes as redividing the chapters and adding verse numbers. President Heber J. Grant called Elder James E. Talmage of the Twelve to prepare the 1920 edition which included double-column pages and many grammatical improvements. All these are no doubt counted as part of the 4,000 changes.

The Scriptures Publication Committee, working under the direction of the First Presidency, prepared the 1981 edition. Some recurring problems were finally settled in that edition. For example, the printer's manuscript referring to the converted Lamanites read "white and delightsome," although the 1840 edition prepared under the direction of Joseph Smith read *"pure and delightsome."* The publication committee had white permanently changed to pure, as Joseph Smith intended it to be.

The changes in the book present little problem to most Latter-day Saints. Even the most ardent anti-Mormons have cited only about a dozen changes as having any doctrinal and historical significance. A close examination shows that even they are not significant. The Book of Mormon was written by prophets, abridged by a prophet, translated by a prophet, and changes were made under the further direction of a prophet. It was the word of God before the changes were made and it is the word of God after the changes have been made.

The changes in the Book of Mormon are actually few compared to the number of changes made in today's English Bibles. The late William Barclay, one of the best known of British Bible expositors, records the following facts:

> In the Greek manuscript of the New Testament, there are 150,000 places in which there are variant readings. Of those 150,000, fewer than 400 affect the sense, fewer than 50 are of any importance (William Barclay, *Introducing the Bible*, p. 134).

Barclay also cites a 19th century committee of the American Bible Society which examined six different editions of the Authorized Version (King James) and found nearly 24,000 differences! (*Ibid,* p. 134)

If the 4,000 minor changes in the Book of Mormon make it without value, what do the 24,000 differences in the Bible do to its worth? Some detractors would probably be aghast if they read about the number of changes to the Bible. Do detractors feel differently about their conviction that the Bible is the word of God because of these changes? We would think not.

For further explanation regarding changes in the Book of Mormon, see:

Ensign, December 1983, pp. 25-28.

Robert Matthews, 'The New Publications of the Standard Works—1979, 1981," *Brigham Young University Studies (BYU Studies),* Vol. 22, No. 4, Fall 1982, pp. 387-424.

Hugh Nibley, *Since Cumorah,* Deseret Book, 1967, pp. 6-7.

Sidney B. Sperry *Answers to Book of Mormon Questions,* Bookcraft, 1967, pp. 183-92; 197-205.

Book of Mormon Critical Text, published by FARMS.

Part 2

Answers to
Questions
About

The
Bible

Notes

13

Can Anyone "Add To It"?

Question: Since Revelation 22:18, 19 says that no man shall add to the Bible, how can Latter-day Saints teach that Joseph Smith or any other man can add to the scriptures?

While Rev. 22:18, 19 forbids man from adding to "the prophecy of this book" [the Book of Revelation], it in no way prevents God or his son, Jesus Christ, from giving additional revelation to man through his prophets.

While the Book of Revelation was placed last in the Bible, Bible scholars agree that it was not the last book of the Bible written. Evidence indicates that 1 John and Jude were written up to 20 years later than Revelation, which is believed to have been written about 90 AD. Many also believe that the Gospel of St. John was written after the Book of Revelation.

Critics seem to forget that the Bible is a *collection* of books. John's Book of Revelation was a single book for centuries before it was assembled with other books to form the Bible. How can critics say Revelation 22 refers to the entire Bible when there was no Bible when Revelation was written, and there would not be one for hundreds of years?

Additionally, in the Old Testament, Deuteronomy 4:2 states that "Ye shall not add unto the word which I command you, neither shall ye diminish ought from it, that ye may keep the commandments of the Lord." Obviously, there are many books in the Bible added after Deuteronomy, including the entire New Testament. In effect, the verses in Revelation and Deuteronomy mean that one is not to add to or take away from the *specific* books of Revelation and Deuteronomy.

The Apostle John records in John 16:12 that the Lord said he had many other things to say, but we couldn't bear them at that time. The same thing is recorded in 3 Nephi 17:2. If Revelation 22:18, 19 forbids God from speaking any more to man as some critics of Latter-day Saints claim, how are these additional words of Christ that John promised going to be revealed?

The Apostle Peter tells us that prophecy comes as holy men of God speak as they are moved by the Holy Ghost (2 Pet. 1:21). As holy men write, these things become scripture. The Church of Jesus Christ of Latter-day Saints agrees with the Lord, as recorded in John 16:12, that Christ has more to reveal to us and that he does it through holy men of God as moved upon by the Holy Ghost (D & C 68:4), and that the result is scripture after it is accepted and canonized by the Church. Thank goodness for a Church that teaches that God still loves us enough to reveal His word to us in our day.

Perhaps the greatest tragedy that occurred during the apostasy was the adoption of the erroneous teachings that the Bible is sufficient, that there is no more need for additional revelation or scripture, and that anyone who claims to have additional revelation is not of God.

14

Was Moroni a False Spirit?

Question: How can Latter-day Saints believe in the Angel Moroni story when Paul warns about an angel from heaven who can transform himself into an angel of light and can deceive even the elect?

It is true that Paul does warn us about false or evil messengers or angels that could deceive us (Gal. 1:6-9; 2 Cor. 11:14), but let us not let two such warnings negate the validity and value of hundreds of true angelic visitors who were sent from God to bless mankind. There are 275 references to angels in the Bible, and only seven of those references have to do with false angels. The fact that Satan *may* appear as an angel of light obviously does not mean that *all* angels that appear to man are of Satan, by any means.

Let us review a handful of the powerful experiences where the visitation of angels was a great blessing to mankind:

- Two angels ate with Lot, blinded the Sodomites, and brought Lot and his family out of Sodom (Gen. 19:1-22).
- The angel of the Lord called to Abraham from heaven, stopped him from sacrificing Isaac, and told him that God would multiply his descendants (Gen. 22:11-18).
- An angel was sent to Daniel and shut the lions' mouths so that they would not hurt him (Dan. 6:22).
- Angels appeared unto Mary and her cousin Elizabeth's husband, Zacharias, foretelling the births of Jesus and John the Baptist. An angel also appeared to Mary's husband, Joseph, on at least two

occasions, keeping him abreast of blessings and dangers (Luke 1:11-38; Matt. 1:18-24, 2:13, 19-23).

- An angel announced the birth of Jesus to the shepherds, and an angel told Mary to name her baby Jesus (Luke 2:8-14; 1:26-38).
- An angel from heaven appeared to Jesus in the garden of Gethsemane and strengthened him (Luke 22:43).
- It was two angels in white apparel who said, "Why stand ye gazing up into heaven? this same Jesus, which is taken up from you into heaven, shall so come in like manner as ye have seen him go into heaven" (Acts 1:11).
- After Christ's death, an angel instructed Cornelius to send for the Apostle Peter, an event which helped broaden the ministry to include Gentiles (Acts 10:1-6). (What would have happened if Cornelius or the Apostles had rationalized that the heavenly being was an angel of Satan? Is an angel only considered Satanic when it carries a message that evangelical Christians do not choose to accept?)
- Paul also had experiences with angels. One appeared to him when he was caught in a storm at sea and assured him that all on board the ship would live and that Paul would be brought before Caesar (Acts 27:23-24).

If the appearance of angels continued after the death and resurrection of Christ, at what point in time would our critics say their appearance became unacceptable? Angels still exist today, and the Lord may use them as he wishes. Indeed, many prophesied events in the Last Days will involve angelic messengers from God.

Angels are "ministering spirits, sent forth to minister for them who shall be heirs of salvation," according to the author of Hebrews (Heb. 1:14). Angels also watch over the churches (Rev. 1:20). Angels will be very much involved when Christ returns. The Son of man shall "send forth his angels, and they shall gather out of his kingdom all things that offend" (Matt. 13:39-41). Angels will be with the Lord when he rewards every man according to his works (Matt. 16:27). Angels will help gather the elect of the earth (Matt. 24:30-31).

These last three examples are of future visitations of Godly angels which will, of course, occur long after Paul wrote his warning. Those who categorize every angel as a messenger from Satan would miss being caught up with Jesus when he comes, rejecting the angels assigned to this task.

The wholesale discounting of appearances of angels based on one or two scriptures in Paul's epistles indicates narrowness of interpretation and may well affect one's openness to receive messengers from Jesus Christ. Unfortunately, a person almost has to adopt that stand if he believes that the heavens are sealed and that there is no further need for revelation from God. Yet the Bible in no way precludes the kind of experiences that Joseph Smith had. In fact, it promises such events in the latter days:

> In the last days, saith God, I will pour out of my Spirit upon all flesh: and your sons and your daughters shall prophesy, and your young men shall see visions, and your old men shall dream dreams (Acts 2:17).

John the Revelator prophesied of the last days, saying, "I saw another angel fly in the midst of heaven, having the everlasting gospel to preach unto them that dwell on the earth, and to every nation, and kindred, and tongue, and people" (Rev. 14:6). Who was this angel of the last days if it was not Moroni?

As shown by the numerous passages listed above, angels and visions are very much a part of the everlasting gospel of Jesus Christ. To deny that and teach otherwise is to preach "another gospel," which Paul also warned about in his epistles (Gal. 1:6-9).

15
Do Latter-day Saints
Teach "Another Gospel"?

Question: Are Latter-day Saints not Christian because they teach another gospel? Paul warned us about such people in Galatians 1:6-9.

A typical response to this accusation is that Latter-day Saints do not teach a different Gospel than was preached by the ancient apostles—it is the various Christian sects who do. But this response is incomplete because the original question is based on an erroneous understanding of Galatians 1:6-9. We should examine this scripture closely and determine who was writing to whom, when, and why.

Paul was writing to the Galatians to warn them about what he perceived as a growing problem within the Church itself. People had entered his flock, attempting to mislead it by preaching another gospel, a perverted one, different from the one that Paul himself had preached to these Gentiles who had just joined the Church.

Who were these people? Were these pagans or some other brand of non-Christians preaching a perverted gospel? It was neither. In fact, they were fellow Christians from the Church at Jerusalem who were trying to solve what they saw as a growing problem among the non-Jewish converts. The brethren from Jerusalem wanted all male converts, Jewish and Gentiles alike, to comply with the requirement of circumcision and to make a commitment to keep the Law of Moses.

Earlier, Paul had been upset when Peter entered Paul's mission field teaching "another gospel"—a gospel of circumcision, while Paul advocated the gospel of uncircumcision (Gal. 2:7). It was Peter who received the vision to widen the ministry to all people, including the Gentiles. This was a marked change from the ministry of Christ, who took his message only to the House of Israel. Yet Peter still wasn't convinced, as evidenced in Galatians 2, that there should be full fellowship with the uncircumcised Christians. Paul therefore referred to what Peter was teaching as another gospel—the gospel of circumcision.

Students of the Bible know that circumcision was a divisive issue in the New Testament church for many years, even after Peter's vision of the "unclean" animals when he was told "what God hath cleansed, that call not thou common" (Acts 10:15-35). This controversy over the gospel of circumcision (Gal. 2:7) caused so much of a disruption in the church that the Apostles once gathered in Jerusalem to resolve the issue and to determine and write their unified position (Acts 15).

But back to Galatians—Paul was upset with Peter, who had been dining with the Gentile Christians until some of the Jewish Christians came into the area. Peter then separated himself from the Gentiles, which was so upsetting to Paul that he "withstood him to the face," or in other words, discussed it openly with Peter at Antioch (Gal. 2:11).

Paul continued to be angered by Peter and certain others who were still preaching the gospel of circumcision to the uncircumcised Gentile Christians. Noted Christian theologian F. F. Bruce adds his comments on the issue Paul was addressing in Galatians chapters 1 and 2:

> If God's redeeming grace was to be received by faith, and not by conformity with the Law of Moses, then it was available on equal terms to Jew and Gentile and to make a distinction in practice between Jewish and Gentile believers, as Peter and the others were doing, was in practice to deny the gospel (*Paul: Apostle of the Heart Set Free,* p. 178).

Galatians 1:6-9 has to do with a specific doctrinal problem confronting the early Christians. To apply this scripture to any other doctrine with which detractors disagree is to wrest the scriptures.

16
Do Latter-day Saints Tear Down the Bible?

Question: Why do Latter-day Saints tear down the Bible?

Latter-day Saints don't tear down the Bible—they hold it in high esteem and regard it as the recorded word of God. However, a few well-meaning members, in an effort to help people sense the importance of the Book of Mormon, have a tendency to elaborate on the books that are missing in the Bible, the Biblical doctrines that are not clear, or they focus on erroneous translations in parts of the Bible, to the exclusion of what is so priceless about the Bible.

Detractors, building on that tendency and trying to bolster their erroneous notion that Latter-day Saints aren't Christian, often attempt to give the impression that Latter-day Saints are anti-Bible. This just isn't true. We believe the Bible is the word of God, and we study it, cherish it, and use it so we may better understand God's will. Joseph Fielding Smith said that the Bible "has had a greater influence on the world for good than any other book ever published."

Regardless, some try to extract the idea that we don't value the Bible from the eighth Article of Faith, which states, "We believe the Bible to be the word of God as far as it is translated correctly." When detractors take this to mean that we feel the Bible is of little worth, the conclusion they draw just isn't true, and it is diametrically opposed to the central message of the Article of Faith they are attempting to explain away. We don't have a problem with the

Bible—only with occasional mistranslated passages found in various Bible translations.

Latter-day Saints do not believe that any one translation of the Bible is without error, but detractors twist this to mean that Mormons do not accept the Bible as the word of God. However, from this author's experience with numerous Christians, Latter-day Saints seem to accept the Bible more literally than all other denominations!

Fundamentalists or Evangelical Christians, which make up the majority of our most vocal detractors, generally believe in the inerrancy of the Bible, which means that they believe it is without error of any kind. The Book of Mormon, while testifying to the truthfulness of the Bible, does inform us that many plain and precious things were purposely taken out of the Bible centuries ago (1 Nephi 13:26-27). Even in the last decade, clerics of some of the more liberal Christian groups have continued to remove precious truths from the Bible. In one of the more recent translations, for instance, some have gone so far as to change the gender of God.

Latter-day Saints generally would agree with Elder Bruce R. McConkie and others who have stated that the Bible is the foremost of the Standard Works of the Church; that it is the first of the accepted, approved, canonized volumes of scripture used by the Saints as a standard by which all doctrine and procedures are judged (*A New Witness for the Articles of Faith,* p. 390).

The LDS Church unwaveringly testifies of the divine nature of the Bible. The Doctrine and Covenants teaches, through a revelation from the Lord found in the 20th Section, that one of the reasons for the coming forth of the Book of Mormon is to prove to the world that "the holy scriptures are true" (D & C 20:11). Obviously, the Lord was speaking of the Bible as the holy scriptures, as it was the only Judeo-Christian scriptures that the world had prior to the coming forth of the Book of Mormon.

While critics sometimes focus on 1 Nephi 13 and its declaration that the plain and precious truths were taken from the Bible, they fail to cite the hundreds of Biblical truths which are testified to by Book of Mormon prophets. These prophets provide a second witness to the truthfulness of such Biblical occurrences as the fall of Adam, the building of the Tower of Babel, and the dividing of the

Red Sea incidents which some Bible scholars doubt. Bible rendi-
tions of miracles, parables, and even the greatest of events—the resurrection of our Savior—are further born witness to in the Book of
Mormon. Clearly the Book of Mormon strengthens the witness of
the Bible rather than weakening it.

When critics do mention any Biblical reference found in the
Book of Mormon, it is usually accompanied by the accusation that
Joseph Smith copied from the Bible. But what could make more
sense than the Lord inspiring additional prophets in later dispensations to testify to his words given to prophets in earlier dispensations? Surely the Book of Mormon is a second witness, not only to
Jesus Christ, but to the truth of the Bible itself.

17

Why Trust in "Burnings in the Bosom"?

Question: Why do Mormons put their trust in a "burning in their bosoms" while real Christians put their trust in the Bible?

If a conviction of truth comes only through reading the Bible, one can't help but wonder why there are so many different Protestant and Catholic churches in the world today.

The Bible teaches that one cannot know that Jesus is the Lord without the Holy Ghost (1 Cor. 12:3), which works on the heart and guides us into all truth (John 16:13). For example, on the day of Pentecost, the three thousand who were led to Jesus, and who joined the Church and were baptized, were not converted by reading the New Testament—it hadn't been written yet. They weren't converted by studying the writing of the ancient prophets either—the Pharisees and Sadducees had been doing that for centuries, yet they didn't accept Christ.

The three thousand were converted because of a pouring out of the Spirit, which bore testimony to them. They were, as the Bible so aptly states, "pricked in their heart" (Acts 2:37). Once the conversion process begins, Paul tells us that God sends forth "the Spirit of his Son "into your hearts" (Gal. 4:6). Does that mean if you do not feel of His Spirit in your heart that you aren't converted? The author believes it does.

Critics are mistaken if they think Latter-day Saints only put their trust in physical sensations in their chests. Perhaps we have focused too much on the earlier phrase of D & C 9:8 where the Lord tells Oliver Cowdery that his "bosom shall burn" within, and we sometimes miss the most important part of that sentence: "you shall feel that it is right."

We have been commanded to "trust in that Spirit which leadeth to do good—yea, to do justly, to walk humbly, to judge righteously; and this is my Spirit" (D & C 11:12). We know that the fruits of this same spirit are "love, joy, peace, longsuffering, gentleness, goodness, faith, meekness, temperance" (Gal. 5:22, 23). It is this Spirit with his many "fruits" of good character that we strive and pray for, not just for a "burning in the bosom."

Nevertheless, the Bible teaches that feelings of the Spirit are often experienced as a burning in the bosom. Two disciples who were on the road to Emmaus were visited by the resurrected Lord. They didn't recognize him with their eyes, nor because of their knowledge of the scriptures. They recognized him when "their eyes were opened" and they recalled: "Did not our heart burn within us, while he talked with us by the way, and while he opened to us the scriptures?" (Luke 24:32)

Alma teaches us that to be born again is a spiritual process that affects the heart and begins as we receive Christ. He asked members of the Church, "Have ye experienced this mighty change in your hearts?" (Alma 5:14). True conversion is an experience of the heart—it can't come solely from reading the Bible, since the Bible as we know it only came into being in the 4th century A.D. Many early Christians died in the Roman Coliseum. Why were they willing to die? Because of a conviction of the heart. For centuries after the Bible canon was formed, Christians still did not have access to it. Many were actually forbidden to read it.

Detractors who are sometimes "past feeling" poke fun at the spiritual feelings of one's heart. They have even likened it to indigestion from too much pizza. Perhaps some have become so numb to feelings of the Spirit that they do not know what it is like to be "pricked in their heart." Instead they mock those who attempt to describe a spiritual event with common words.

18

Why Believe In It Only "As It Is Translated Correctly"?

Question: Doesn't it show a lack of faith in the Bible to declare that you only believe it as far as it is translated correctly?

What is the alternative? Would it be more correct to say, "We believe the Bible to be the word of God whether or not it is translated correctly," or "We believe the Bible to be the word of God even if it "is translated incorrectly"? It has never failed to amaze the author that someone could take issue with the eighth LDS Article of Faith, which states in part that "We believe the Bible to be the word of God as far as it is translated correctly." To take another view would imply that incorrect Bible translations are acceptable or that no translation has ever had an error in it. Both of these are naive positions. Joseph Smith discussed this concern when he said:

> I believe the Bible as it read when it came from the pen of the original writers. Ignorant translators, careless transcribers, or designing and corrupt priests have committed many errors (*History of the Church,* Vol. 6, p. 57).

The concern, as can be seen by such statements, is not only that there be a faithful translation, but that there also be a faithful transmission of the original Biblical text. Non-LDS scholars are in agreement that the Biblical texts have undergone a variety of modifications:

> The early manuscripts were all copied by hand, and in the copying, changes and errors crept in. It has been calculated that in the Greek manuscripts of the New Testament there are 150,000 places in which there are variant readings (*Introducing the Bible,* pp. 133-34).

While many of these variants are minor (spelling, word order etc.), they nevertheless pose difficulties for translators who try to determine the original text of the New Testament. Complicating the problem of translation is the fact that there are no known original manuscripts of the Old or New Testament which exist today. Translators are therefore, unable to compare later manuscripts with originals.

Some changes in the Biblical text were not just copying errors, but intentional alterations. Noted textual experts such as Bruce Metzger have observed:

> Many of the alterations which may be classified as intentional were no doubt introduced in good faith by copyists who believed that they were correcting an error or infelicity of language which had previously crept into the sacred text and needed to be rectified. A later scribe might even reintroduce an erroneous reading that had been previously corrected (*The Text of the New Testament,* p. 195).

Metzger further added:

> The number of deliberate alterations made in the interests of doctrine is difficult to assess. Irenaeus, Clement of Alexandria, Tertullian and many other Church Fathers accused the heretics of corrupting the scriptures in order to have support for their special views (*Ibid.,* p. 201).

Perhaps the best-known example of this is the statement in 1 John 5:7-8:

> For there are three that bear record in heaven, the Father, the Word, and the Holy Ghost: and these three are one.
> And there are three that bear witness in earth, the Spirit, and the water, and the blood: and these three agree in one.

This is a spurious text appearing nowhere in earlier New Testament manuscripts. This fact is attested to by numerous scholars who declare that it was apparently a marginal note included as part of the manuscript text.

Latter-day Saints recognize the Bible as the word of God and accept it as their foremost book of scripture. They also recognize that it has undergone a series of changes, and therefore reserve the right to believe it to be God's word as far as it has been translated and transmitted correctly.

Part 3

Answers to
Questions
About

Joseph
Smith

Notes

19

Did He Claim To Do a Greater Work Than Jesus?

Question: How can Latter-day Saints follow a man who boasts to have done a greater work than Jesus Christ?

The detractors are referring to a statement Joseph Smith delivered in Nauvoo, Illinois, in May, 1844, shortly before his death. It is true that he was boasting, having patterned his address after a talk by Paul recorded in 2 Corinthians, chapter 11. In that sermon, Paul the Apostle was doing some boasting of his own to the Gentiles. Joseph Smith picked up on Paul's theme when he said,

> I have more to boast of than any man had. I am the only man that has ever been able to keep a whole church together since the days of Adam. A large majority of the whole have stood by me. Neither Paul, John, Peter, nor Jesus ever did it. I boast that no man ever did such work as I (*History of the Church*, Vol. 6, pp. 408-09).

While we aren't sure this is a completely accurate quote, let us assume that it is. Detractors read into this statement that the Prophet was saying he did a greater work than Jesus Christ. Considering the entire text and the circumstance of the time, he seems to be saying only that he was able to keep the Church together better than others did, including Jesus Christ.

Surely Joseph Smith would be the first to agree that keeping a church together is not a greater or a more significant work than what was done by Jesus. There is nothing as significant as being the God of Israel, taking upon oneself the sins of the world, dying for all mankind that they might live, nor being resurrected. Surely, everlasting life is the greatest gift anyone could give.

Nevertheless, the Lord himself said, "Verily, verily, I say unto you, He that believeth on me, the works that I do shall he do also; and greater works than these shall he do; because I go unto my Father" (John 14:12). To what greater work could the Savior be referring? Perhaps the Lord means a larger work, but certainly not more significant. For example, John the Baptist presumably baptized more people than Jesus, Paul may have converted more as a missionary, Moses led more Israelites out of bondage, Noah built a bigger ship, and Joseph Smith kept the Church together longer.

The point should be clear: if greater means quantity, there are many who fulfilled the Savior's promise that his followers would do "greater works," and this includes Joseph Smith.

20

Did He Falsely Prophesy of Christ's Return?

Question: Didn't Joseph Smith prophesy that Christ would return in 1890?

First of all, the Savior, while here on earth, told us that no one on earth knows when the Lord will return: "But of that day and hour knoweth no man, no, not the angels of heaven, but my Father only" (Matt. 24:36). Because we do not know, we need to constantly be ready for his return, for "in such an hour as ye think not the Son of Man cometh" (Matt. 24:44).

However, Joseph Smith did make several interesting statements about seeing the Savior. One of them is a favorite of our detractors. They have misquoted it, misreported it, misinterpreted it, and mis-explained it. Most often they simply do not complete the quote, making it appear that the prophet said something he didn't.

The passage in question is found in Section 130 of the Doctrine and Covenants. It is reported in abbreviated form, and Joseph acknowledged as he recorded it that he didn't understand the meaning or intent of the revelation. Joseph Smith recorded:

> I was once praying very earnestly to know the time of the coming of the Son of Man, when I heard a voice repeat the following:

Joseph, my son, if thou livest until thou art eighty-five years old, thou shalt see the face of the Son of Man; therefore let this suffice, and trouble me no more on this matter. (D & C 130:14-15)

Many of our detractors end the quote at this point, and then they assume that the statement is a prophecy that the Savior would come in the year 1890 or 1891, since the prophet Joseph was born in 1805. However, if the reader will continue further in that passage, he will see that Joseph Smith himself stated:

I was left thus, without being able to decide whether this coming referred to the beginning of the millennium or to some previous appearing, or whether I should die and thus see his face (D & C 130:16).

We only learn what the prophet did prophesy by reading verse 17: "I believe the coming of the Son of Man will not be any sooner than that time." Without a doubt, that prophecy came true. The Lord did not return to the earth for His Second Coming before that time.

But there are other aspects of fulfillment that should also be considered. We do not know when it was that the Prophet earnestly prayed to know the time of the Lord's coming. The context, (verse 13), shows that it may have taken place in 1832 or earlier. At least twice, as is recorded in the Doctrine and Covenants, Joseph saw the face of the Son of Man. D & C 76:20-24 and D & C 110:2-10 both record appearances of the Lord Jesus Christ, either of which may constitute fulfillment of the Lord's prophetic promise. He may also have seen the Lord's face at the time of his death in 1844, as he pondered in D & C 130:16.

Joseph made reference to the incident on at least two other occasions, and indicated that his belief was not that the Lord *would come* by the time of his 85th birthday, but rather that the Lord *would not come* before that time, which of course was a correct prophecy.

In the *History of the Church,* Vol. 5, pp. 336-37, the words of the prophet are recorded on the subject: "I prophesy in the name of the Lord God, and let it be written—the Son of Man will not come in the clouds of heaven till I am eighty-five years old." Again, Joseph Smith doesn't say the Lord will come then, but that He *will not come before* that time.

In another place in the *History of the Church,* Vol. 6, p. 254, Joseph Smith again prophesied on the subject of Christ's coming:

> I also prophesy, in the name of the Lord, that Christ will not come in forty years; and if God ever spoke by my mouth, He will not come in that length of time. Brethren, when you go home, write this down, that it may be remembered.
>
> Jesus Christ never did reveal to any man the precise time that He would come. Go and read the Scriptures, and you cannot find anything that specifies the exact hour He would come; and all that say so are false teachers.

If this prophecy is read carefully, instead it being an "unfulfilled prophecy" as asserted by the detractors, it actually testifies to the truthfulness of the mission and prophetic stature of the Prophet Joseph Smith. No man knows the exact time the Savior will return, and Joseph Smith never claimed to.

21

Can People Go to Heaven Without His Consent?

Question: How can Latter-day Saints claim to worship Jesus Christ when their leaders teach that no one will get to heaven without the consent or passport of Joseph Smith (Journal of Discourses, Vol. 7, p. 289, 1869)?

Many traditional Christians envision Peter standing at the "pearly gates." They are uncomfortable with the misunderstanding that Brigham Young said Joseph Smith will take Peter's place. The thoughtful reader, however, will search the entire discourse delivered by Brigham Young and see that this is not what he was teaching.

Each dispensation has a prophet at its head. Moses taught in his dispensation that those who looked to the serpent on a pole would live. This was a type (Alma 33:19) or similitude of the Savior. Those who didn't obey Moses and would not look, didn't live. Accepting what Moses said in that dispensation was the "passport" to life.

As Christ said:

Do not think that I will accuse you to the Father: there is one that accuseth you, even Moses, in whom ye trust.

For had ye believed Moses, ye would have believed me: for he wrote of me.

But if ye believe not his writings, how shall ye believe my words? (John 5:45-47)

If they didn't believe in Moses, he wasn't their "passport."

Noah offered "salvation" to those who would join him in the ark. Those who were disobedient and failed to enter the ark were swept off the earth in the flood and ended up in spirit prison (1 Peter 3:20). Again, as the prophet of his dispensation, Noah provided the "passport" for those who accepted the word of God that came through him.

In the meridian of time, those who accepted the apostles and prophets and did not reject the message of Jesus Christ were saved. As the Lord said to the apostles, "He that receiveth you receiveth me" (Matt. 10:40).

While speaking about our own dispensation, Brigham Young said that people of this dispensation will not enter God's Kingdom without the "consent" and "certificate" of Joseph Smith as a passport to entering where God and Christ are. Brigham Young then explained what he meant: "It is his [Joseph's] mission to see that all the children of men in this last dispensation are saved, that can be, through the redemption" (*Journal of Discourses,* vol. 7, p. 289).

The "passport," then, that people will need to enter heaven is the same as they have always needed, no matter what dispensation they lived in. To accept Christ is to accept his prophets: without the priesthood authority and inspired teachings of the Lord that have come through Joseph Smith, no one in this dispensation, living or dead, can be redeemed.

Anti-Mormon critics distort this view, trying to make it appear that Joseph Smith will be standing by the gate of heaven admitting or rejecting those who seek to enter. This is not the picture that is painted by Brigham Young. He was merely stating that the mission of Joseph Smith, God's prophet, was "to see that all the children of men in the last dispensation are saved, that can be through the redemption."

It should be recognized that the Savior is a great delegator. He has delegated to the "head" of each dispensation certain responsibilities, including some preliminary judging responsibilities. For example, in New Testament times the Apostles were told that they will judge the twelve tribes of Israel (Matt 19:28). Literally, then, those of the Twelve Tribes won't "get to Heaven" without the consent of the Apostles.

Latter-day Saints do not believe Joseph Smith is the keeper of the gate of heaven, nor the one who determines whether we are saved. Some Christians think they will instead meet Peter at the "pearly gates," but The Book of Mormon teaches who will really be the final "gatekeeper":

> O then, my beloved brethren, come unto the Lord, the Holy One. Remember that his paths are righteous. Behold, the way for man is narrow, but it lieth in a straight course before him, and the keeper of the gate is the Holy One of Israel; and he employeth no servant there; and there is none other way save it be by the gate; for he cannot be deceived, for the Lord God is his name (2 Nephi 9:41).

22
Did He Falsely Prophesy of a Temple in Independence?

Question: *If Joseph Smith was a prophet of God, how could the Lord tell him that the temple would be built in Independence, Missouri before this generation shall pass away (D & C 84:5)? Surely people aren't still alive who were living in 1832.*

The point most detractors are trying to make with this prophecy is that the generation Joseph Smith spoke of must have passed away by now. Therefore, they would have us believe that makes Joseph Smith a false prophet. But their assertion depends entirely on definition of the word "generation."

Through the length of a literal generation has occasionally been discussed by scholars and has been described as between 25 years to 120 years, in the larger sense, "generation" is often used to describe a gospel dispensation or era. Therefore, no one can be certain how long it will be before the temple is to be completed.

In D & C 124:49, 51 the Lord explains why the temple wasn't built earlier. He said that if

> their enemies come upon them and hinder them from performing that work, behold, it behooveth me to require that work no more at the hands of those sons of men, but to accept of their offerings. . . .
>
> Therefore, for this cause have I accepted the offerings of those whom I commanded to build up a city and a house unto my

name, in Jackson county, Missouri, and were hindered by their enemies, saith the Lord your God.

The Lord did not require the Saints of the 1830s to build the temple in Missouri, but he also did not retract his declaration that it would "be reared in this generation" (D & C 84:4). We simply do not know the length of that generation, and we have good reason to assume that this temple will yet be built.

However, the prophecy in D & C 84:5-6 came to pass less than four years after Joseph Smith received it. Verse 5 states that "this generation shall not all pass away until an house shall be built unto the Lord." The use of words "*an* house" indicate that the Lord is not necessarily referring to "*the* temple" mentioned in verse 4. Additionally, the last mention of a temple in Missouri is in verse 4, with the remaining 116 verses making no mention of it. Anti-Mormon critics are apparently unaware that by verses 5 and 6, the Lord had begun talking about temples and priesthood in general. The "house" mentioned in verse 5 was dedicated in Kirtland, Ohio, in 1836. "A bright light like a pillar of fire" rested upon it, and the glory of the Lord filled the temple, manifested by the abundant presence of the Spirit (*History of the Church,* vol. 2, p. 428) and many journals of the Saints who were in the Kirtland area during the weeks surrounding the temple dedication show that this prophecy was fulfilled in every sense with repeated visitations of the Savior and of angelic beings, and the receipt of numerous visions and other spiritual gifts.

So in reality, D & C 84 is further proof that Joseph Smith was speaking for the Lord, not prophesying falsely as some would accuse.

The remaining question, then, isn't really whether a generation has passed, but whether the Lord can say something will happen that doesn't, or more accurately, whether the Lord ever commands something and then revokes that command. The Doctrine & Covenants records the Lord's' warning that "I, the Lord, command and revoke, as it seemeth me good; and all this to be answered upon the heads of the rebellious, saith the Lord" (D & C 56:4).

One Biblical example of the Lord telling a prophet that something would happen that didn't come to pass can be found in

2 Kings 20:1-7. Here the prophet Isaiah visited Hezekiah, who was "sick unto death," and said to him, "Thus saith the Lord, Set thine house in order; for thou shalt die, and not live." Hezekiah, in prayer, reminded the Lord of all of his good works. The Lord then responded mercifully to his plea. He changed his mind and instructed Isaiah to go back to Hezekiah and tell him that his prayers had been heard; the Lord would heal him and he would live for fifteen more years. Was Isaiah any less a prophet of God because the Lord told him something would happen, and it didn't, for whatever reason?

Another example of the fulfillment of a revealed prophecy being changed is found in Jonah, chapter 3. Here the Lord told Jonah to inform the people of Nineveh that the city would be overthrown in forty days. Then God, it is recorded in verse 10, "Saw their works, that they turned from their evil way; and God repented of the evil, that he had said that he would do unto them; and he did it not (Jonah 3:10).

23

Was He Really a Martyr?

Question: How can Latter-day Saints believe Joseph Smith died as a martyr? All he really did is lose a gun fight at Carthage Jail and killed two men before he died.

Anti-Mormons continue to put unorthodox spins on words such as "Christian," "trinity," and now "martyr." Webster's New World Dictionary defines "martyr" as a person who chooses to suffer or die rather than give up his faith or his principles, or a person tortured or killed because of his beliefs. There is nothing in this definition to prohibit a martyr from defending himself.

Joseph Smith certainly fits this definition of a martyr. To say differently is to either invent a new definition or to be ignorant of the facts regarding the last few days of the prophet's life.

On June 23,1844, Joseph and Hyrum Smith were on the Iowa side of the river on their way to the Great Basin. Orrin P. Rockwell and Reynolds Cahoon carried a message from Emma requesting that Joseph return to Nauvoo (*History of the Church,* Vol. 6, p. 549). Joseph Smith replied to their requests with, "If my life is of no value to my friends it is of none to myself" (p. 549).

Before returning to Nauvoo later that same evening, he made a statement that he would repeat several times in the next few days. He declared that if he and Hyrum returned "we shall be butchered" (p. 550). Yet regardless of his foreknowledge of his pending death, that afternoon he, Hyrum and others started back. While some of the party were in a hurry to return to Nauvoo, Joseph said, "It is of no use to hurry, for we are going back to be slaughtered" (p. 551). Obviously, the prophet knew the fate that was awaiting him, yet he chose to "be killed because of his beliefs" rather than to escape death, which he could have easily done.

The next morning a reported 200 people were at Joseph's home in Nauvoo, wanting to see the prophet one more time and to give him their support before he left for Carthage. His mother is reported to have asked him to promise her that he would return, as he had promised during other times of trial. There was no such assurance from the prophet on this occasion.

On the way to Carthage later in the day, the party stopped at the farm of Albert G. Fellow, four miles west of Carthage, where Joseph Smith uttered these fateful words:

> I am going like a lamb to the slaughter, but I am calm as a summer's morning. I have a conscience void of offense toward God and toward all men. If they take my life I shall die an innocent man, and my blood shall cry from the ground for vengeance, and it shall be said of me 'He was murdered in cold blood!' (p. 555).

June 27th found the prophet, his brother Hyrum, John Taylor, and Willard Richards in jail without the protection Governor Ford had promised. At a little after 5 p.m., a mob stormed up the stairs, forced the cell door open and began firing into the room as others fired in the window. After Hyrum fell a "dead man," and as John Taylor was hit several times with flying bullets, Joseph Smith discharged his six shooter into the stairway. His bullets struck three men. Here the historical account is cloudy; some accounts say two men later died, but this conclusion is not certain.

We do know that Joseph Smith and his elder brother Hyrum were killed and John Taylor was seriously wounded, having been shot four times. Willard Richards, eyewitness to the event, remained unharmed. He told of the dreadful incident.

If a martyr is a person who chooses to suffer or die rather than give up his faith or his principles, Joseph Smith fits this definition as well as any other person who has ever been slain.

> He lived great, and he died great in the eyes of God and his people, and like most of the Lord's anointed in ancient times, has sealed his mission and his works with his own blood—and so has his brother Hyrum. In life they were not divided, and in death they were not separated (p. 630).

24
Did He Teach That the Moon Was Inhabited?

Question: Didn't Joseph Smith teach that the moon is inhabited?

The idea that Joseph taught the moon is inhabited comes from the writing of Oliver B. Huntington in 1881 (his journal) and in 1892 (the *Young Woman's Journal*). Huntington claimed that Joseph Smith's father had given him a patriarchal blessing in 1837 which promised that he would preach the gospel to the moon inhabitants.

Close examination reveals that Huntington was only ten years old when he was given this blessing and that his recollections were made over fifty years later. Also, it turns out that the blessing was given by his own father, not Joseph Smith's father.

According to a copy of the blessing in the Church archives (*Blessing Book,* vol. 9, pp. 294-95), it was only one of many given the same day at the same meeting, and none were recorded in detail at the time. Orson Pratt took sketchy notes as the blessings were given, then filled in details later by consulting those who were there. An examination of the blessing shows that the recorded blessing was much more vague than Huntington remembered.

It also appears that Huntington may have picked up on a rumor that Joseph Smith had given a description of the inhabitants of the moon. This description, which Huntington recorded in his journal, is the original source of the anti-Mormon claim that Joseph described the moon inhabitants. Because his journal is also cited in a Young Woman's publication of the Church, it supposedly gives more credibility to the critics.

The statement, which appeared in a two-page article by Oliver B. Huntington entitled "The Inhabitants of the Moon" in the *Young Woman's Journal,* is as follows:

> As far back as 1837, I know that he [Joseph Smith] said the moon was inhabited by men and women the same as this earth, and that they lived to a greater age than we do—that they live generally to near the age of a 1,000 years.
>
> He described the men as averaging nearly six feet in height, and dressing quite uniformly in something near the Quaker style (*Young Woman's Journal,* Vol. 3, p. 263).

From what is quoted here, the most we can conclude is that O. B. Huntington was familiar with rumors of statements that were attributed to Joseph Smith. However, there is nothing in the writings of Joseph Smith or those who recorded his words prior to his death that even hints of any of these views about inhabitants on the moon. This earliest recollection was recorded in 1881, 37 years after the prophet's death.

Even if it turned out that the prophet held these views, nowhere does scripture suggest that a prophet is not allowed to speculate about things that haven't been revealed. Many people during the Nineteenth Century, both the learned and not-so-learned, were speculating on this subject. Joseph Smith's personal opinions and what he taught as revealed doctrine, however, are two entirely different things. The idea that he taught it as a revealed doctrine is based upon Oliver B. Huntington's fifty-year-old, correct or incorrect memory of his blessing, and a rumor that was current in 1881.

Another aspect of the matter needs to be considered. At the present time, man has no scientific or revealed knowledge of whether or not there are inhabitants on the earth's moon. The fact that a handful of astronauts didn't see any inhabitants in the tiny area they viewed when they landed on the moon decades ago certainly gives no definitive information, any more than visitors to earth who might land in barren Death Valley would have any idea of the billions of inhabitants elsewhere.

John the Revelator "saw an angel standing in the sun" (Rev. 19:17). Perhaps we have much to learn about inhabitants of other heavenly spheres.

For further information see Van Hale, "How Could a Prophet Believe in Moonmen?" Mormon Miscellaneous Response Series #4.

82

25

Why Did He Make Changes In the Doctrine & Covenants?

Question: Don't *changes in the revelations in the Doctrine and* Covenants *prove Joseph Smith was not a prophet of God?*

If one compares the 1833 *Book of Commandments* with the current edition of the *Doctrine and Covenants,* one will discover various textual differences. Along with the doctrinally insignificant spelling, grammatical and punctuation changes, one will encounter places where words, or even whole paragraphs, have been added.

These additions sometimes required deletions and alterations for the added material to mesh properly with the previously existing material. Critics of the Church insist that the only possible explanation for these changes in the revelations is that Joseph Smith was not a true prophet of God.

To assess the validity of this viewpoint, it is necessary to examine the question: Can a true prophet of God add to a God-given revelation? If the answer is "yes," then the fact that Joseph Smith expanded some of the revelations he received is evidence for, not against his prophetic calling. Since we don't have the original manuscripts used for the books of the Bible, nor do we have records of their writing processes, critics cannot claim that Biblical prophets never revised nor added to their revelations—they have no proof. However, the Bible contains an example of the prophet Jeremiah adding to a previously written revelation:

And Baruch wrote from the mouth of Jeremiah all the words of the Lord, which he had spoken unto him, upon a roll of a book (Jer. 36:4).

This revelation was read to King Jehoiakim, who didn't like what he heard:

And it came to pass, that when Jehudi had read three or four leaves, he [King Jehoiakim] cut it with the penknife, and cast it into the fire that was on the hearth, until all the roll was consumed in the fire . . . (Jer. 36:23).

Jeremiah was then instructed by the Lord to rewrite the revelation, which he did. But he did more than simply recreate what Jehoiakim had destroyed:

Then took Jeremiah another roll, and gave it to Baruch the scribe, the son of Neriah; who wrote therein from the mouth of Jeremiah all the words of the book which Jehoiakim king of Judah had burned in the fire: and there were added besides unto them many like words (Jer. 36:32).

If Jeremiah's additions to the destroyed revelation do not disqualify him as a true prophet of God, neither do Joseph Smith's additions disqualify him. Conversely, if Joseph Smith is rejected as a true prophet of God because he added to previously given revelation, Jeremiah should be rejected for the same reason.

Having said this much, the question may be asked, "Why were changes made in the revelations in the first place?" Many revelations were first published in the LDS newspaper, *The Evening and Morning Star,* in Jackson County, Missouri, in 1833. *The Book of Commandments* was published in the same place in the same year. While a comparison shows the revelations to be identical in both of these publications, many changes were made for a reprinting of the *Star.* The reason for the changes were thus explained:

In the first 14 numbers, in the Revelations, are many errors, typographical, and others, occasioned by transcribing manuscript; but as we shall have access to originals, we shall endeavor to make proper corrections (*Evening and Morning Star,* Vol H, No. 24, Sept. 1834, p. 199).

While discussing the substitution of "code names" for people and places in some of the revelations, Orson Pratt remarked:

> But what the Prophet did in relation to this thing, was not of himself: he was dictated by the Holy Ghost to make these substitutions. . . . That he was thus inspired is certain from the fact, that at the very time that he made these substitutions, he also received much additional light; and by revelation line was added upon line to several of the sections and paragraphs about to be published. But some may inquire, are not the Almighty's revelations perfect when they are first given? And if so, where was the propriety of the Lord's adding anything to them; when they were already perfect? We reply that every word of God is perfect; but He does not reveal all things at once but adds 'line upon line, precept upon precept, here a little, and there a little,' revealing as the people are able to bear, or as circumstances require (*The Seer,* Vol. H, No. 3, March 1854, p. 228.

Joseph made some additional changes before the revelations were printed in the Doctrine and Covenants. Again, what Joseph Smith did is in full agreement with Biblical precedent.

26
Did He Prophesy Falsely Regarding David Patten?

Question: Why did Joseph Smith prophesy that David Patten would go on a mission (D & C 114:1), yet six months later Patten was dead? Isn't this just another example of a false prophet making a false prophecy?

D & C 114 was not a prophecy, it was a mission call. Joseph Smith, under the inspiration of the Lord, issued a call for David Patten to go on a mission the following spring. This call by revelation is not a prophecy that David *would* serve a mission, but an admonition to set all his affairs in order so that he *may* perform a mission. Although Patten was killed, his affairs were in order when he died so that his family could endure his absence. This alone indicates the Lord's foreknowledge of Patten's death. And who knows but that Patten served that mission call on the other side of the veil?

In any event, Patten's death would not change the instructional nature of that call. Joseph Smith declared that: To the "great Jehovah . . . the past, present, and future were and are, with Him, one eternal 'now'" (*History of the Church,* Vol. 4, p. 597). The Savior does know all that will happen to us individually, but he still gives agency to us and to others who impact on our lives, which usage often precludes what would have happened if the Lord's will were done on earth as it is in heaven.

There are several Biblical parallels to David Patten's mission call, such as the calling of Judas as an Apostle. As one of the Twelve

Apostles, Judas was promised by the Lord that he would sit on twelve thrones with the others and judge the twelve tribes of Israel (Matt. 19:28). Judas, of his own choice (unlike David Patten) never fulfilled this promise of the Lord. This doesn't make the Lord a false prophet in the case of Judas. Nor were the Lord and His prophet, Joseph Smith, mistaken in the case of David Patten.

The Lord knocks at the door and gives the promise or opportunity. Whether we open the door and respond in a way to reap the potential blessing is up to us, and in many cases, up to the righteousness of others. In David Patten's case, extenuating circumstances prevented him from serving an earthly mission: a mob killed him.

To understand the case of David Patten, one might study D & C 124:49, which states if "their enemies come upon them and hinder them from performing that work, behold, it behooveth me to require that work no more at the hands of those sons of men, but to accept of their offerings."

Part 4

Answers to Questions About

Church Doctrine

Notes

27

How Does Baptism Relate to Being "Born Again"?

Question: Don't Latter-day Saints believe that being born again is the same as baptism and confirmation?

A statement from the late Apostle Bruce R. McConkie shows the difference between being baptized and being born again:

> Mere compliance with the formality of the ordinance of baptism does not mean that a person has been born again. No one can be born again without baptism, but the immersion in water and the laying on of hands to confer the Holy Ghost do not of themselves guarantee that a person has been or will be born again (*Mormon Doctrine*, 2nd ed., pp. 100-01).

What is meant by being born again, or spiritual rebirth? Jesus told Nicodemus, "Verily, verily, I say unto thee, Except a man be born again, he cannot see the kingdom of God" (John 3:3). He then added, "Verily, verily, I say unto thee, Except a man be born of water and of the Spirit, he cannot enter into the kingdom of God" (v. 5). Here, Jesus is making it clear that for the rebirth to occur at least two things must happen: a person must be born of water (baptism) and be born of the Spirit (Holy Ghost). These steps enable us to become, in effect, newborn babes in Christ (1 Peter 1:3; 2:2).

The Book of Mormon speaks a great deal about this rebirth that must take place for salvation to occur:

And the Lord said unto me: Marvel not that all mankind, yea, men and women, all nations, kindreds, tongues and people, must be born again; yea, born of God, changed from their carnal and fallen state, to a state of righteousness, being redeemed of God, becoming his sons and daughters;

And thus they become new creatures; and unless they do this, they can in nowise inherit the Kingdom of God (Mosiah 27:25-26).

When an individual becomes aware of his own weaknesses and his dependence on Christ for salvation, he makes a covenant to follow Christ. The emerging new creature is seen as a new person, the offspring of Christ, being spiritually reborn:

And now, because of the covenant which ye have made ye shall be called the children of Christ, his sons, and his daughters; for behold, this day he hath spiritually begotten you; for ye say that your hearts are changed through faith on his name; therefore, ye are born of him and have become his sons and his daughters (Mosiah 5:7).

The late Apostle Mark E. Petersen describes the rebirth:

Unless a man is born again, he cannot see the Kingdom of God. I do not believe that a person will ever see the Kingdom of God unless he is born again . . . that birth of the spirit means something more than most of us normally realize. Through proper teaching, a conviction is born in our soul. Faith develops, through it we see how important it is to become like Christ. We see ourselves as we are in contrast to a Christlike soul. A desire for a change-over is born within us. The change-over begins. We call it repentance (Address to Seminary and Institute of Religion Personnel, BYU, July 11, 1956).

The late Prophet, David O. McKay indicated:

No man can sincerely resolve to apply to his daily life the teachings of Jesus of Nazareth without sensing a change in his own nature. The phrase, "born again," has a deeper significance than many attach to it. This changed feeling may be indescribable, but it is real. Happy the person who has truly sensed the uplifting, transforming power that comes from this nearness to the Savior, this kinship to the Living Christ (*Conference Report,* April 1962, p. 7).

The rebirth is a very personal, spiritual experience which usually follows water baptism and reception of the gift of the Holy Ghost. In fact, we have no New Testament account of individuals being "born again" until after they had been baptized by water.

While the second birth conceivably may occur at the same time one is baptized into the Kingdom, it usually occurs some time after, as one continues to hunger and thirst for the companionship of the Spirit. Only on rare occasions does a birth of the Spirit occur before baptism, as was the case with King Lamoni (Alma 19:33-35) and the Lamanites taught by Lehi and Nephi (Hel. 5:20-52). They were, however, baptized soon thereafter.

Spiritual birth is an experience shared by those who are seeking the Christlike life and who have the hope of salvation. Water baptism for Latter-day Saints is one of several essential components of the rebirth process, not the completion.

28

Can Men Become As God?

Question: Why do Latter-day Saints perpetuate the same lie that the devil told Adam and Eve, that "ye shall be as gods"?

Critics are right, the devil did lie in the Garden of Eden; but he mixed his lie with truth. Let us read the text and see what God said would happen to Adam if he partook of the tree of the knowledge of good and evil, then compare it to what the devil said would happen. Then we will see what God observed after the forbidden fruit was eaten.

The account in question is found in Chapter 2 of Genesis, verses 16 and 17:

> And the Lord God commanded the man, saying, Of every tree of the garden thou mayest freely eat;
> But of the tree of the knowledge of good and evil, thou shalt not eat of it: for in the day that thou eatest thereof thou shalt surely die.
> The beast, or the devil, then entered the garden and talked to Eve.

In Genesis 3:4-5 we read:

> And the serpent said unto the woman, Ye shall not surely die:
> For God doth know that in the day ye eat thereof, then your eyes shall be opened, and ye shall be as gods, knowing good and evil.

In this passage we see that the serpent truly did mix truth and falsehood. He told one lie and two truths:

1. your eyes shall be opened, (true)
2. you shall be as gods, knowing good and evil, (true)
3. ye shall not surely die, (lie)

Adam and Eve then ate of the fruit of the tree. What happened? Just as the devil said, their eyes were opened; they realized they were naked and hid. Then, just as the devil had said, they became as one of the Gods. Verse 22 relates the word of God confirming that this portion of the serpent's statement was true, not a lie: "And the Lord God said, Behold the man is become as one of us to know good and evil."

However, Adam and Eve were then cast out of the Garden of Eden and out of God's presence; therefore they died spiritually and would someday die physically. So, Adam and Eve did die, just the opposite of what the devil said. This was Satan's lie. Yet in perfect plainness, the scriptures show us that the other things Satan told them were true. Critics are certainly quick to point out that the devil said we could become as gods. Do they not know that God verified this in verse 22?

A beautiful reminder of our ability to ultimately become as God is found in John 10:34-36:

> Jesus answered them, Is it not written in your law, I said, *Ye are Gods?*
>
> If he called them *gods, unto whom the word of God came,* and the scripture cannot be broken;
>
> Say ye of him, whom the Father hath sanctified, and sent into the world, Thou blasphemest; because I said, I am the Son of God?

29

Are All Statements By LDS Authorities Doctrine?

Question: Is everything said by LDS Church leaders to be regarded as sound doctrine and therefore binding on the Church?

Anti-Mormon critics often rummage through hundreds of pages of Church history or lectures by General Authorities of the last 160 years to find some statement they regard as doctrinally unsound or emotionally inflammatory, hoping to embarrass the Church by what was said then. These critics then try to use these "tidbits" as leverage against Latter-day Saints who might, in error, believe that everything said by General Authorities is Church doctrine and therefore binding on the Church and its members.

It is, of course, unfair to hold the Church responsible for every statement, true or false, made by any one of its members. The member who made the statement in question must be the one held responsible for the statement.

A double standard is used by these anti-Mormon critics. They would never dream of holding the Lutheran Church responsible for every statement made by Martin Luther, or the Methodist Church responsible for all of John Wesley's remarks. Yet many try to hold the LDS Church responsible for all of its early leaders' remarks, as well as any statement by present leaders. The double standard is compounded because their churches have no apostles nor prophets. They have no one who is recognized as authorized to speak for them. Televangelists, pastors, authors and other individuals express a wide spectrum of personal views. But does anyone expect them to be "authorized spokesmen" for "orthodox Christianity"? Of course not. But the double standard detractors attempt to impose on Latter-day Saints tries to make any member or leader an "official spokesman" of the Church's doctrine, practices and beliefs.

Those doctrines for which the LDS Church is responsible and which are binding upon its members are (1) those which are found in its Standard Works—that is the reason we refer to them as our "Standard Works"; and (2) the official statements approved by the First Presidency and the Quorum of the Twelve Apostles, issued to the Church as doctrine.

Church President Harold B. Lee gave some timeless council in 1972:

> I say that we need to teach our people to find their answers in the scriptures. If only each of us would be wise enough to say that we aren't able to answer any question unless we can find a doctrinal answer in the scriptures! And if we hear someone teaching something that is contrary to what is in the scriptures, each of us may know whether the things spoken are false—it is as simple as that. But the unfortunate thing is that so many of us are not reading the scriptures. We do not know what is in them, and therefore we speculate about the things that we ought to have found in the scriptures themselves. I think that therein is one of our biggest dangers of today (*Ensign*, Dec. 1972, p. 3).

While President Lee was specifically speaking about members using commentaries and other books in place of the scriptures, his advice is equally applicable to sermons, talks, and general responses to issues of the day, no matter where, when, or by whom spoken.

When judging whether something said is reliable or not, we must first view it in light of our Standard Works. We believe in the doctrine of infallibility as it pertains to God, not as it pertains to man. There is only one exception to the rule that everything that is taught should be rooted in the scriptures, and that exception is the prophet. He has the right and responsibility to receive new revelation beyond what has already been revealed in the scriptures.

If a historical tidbit seems inflammatory, we should read it in context with the time, setting, and conditions under which it was said. For example, comments of the brethren regarding the clergy shortly after the death of Joseph Smith at Carthage obviously do not represent the feelings of the Church leadership in the less-emotional times of today. Brigham Young's comments about the government of the United States, while U.S. troops were on the way to Salt Lake City to put down what they thought was the "Mormon Rebellion," must be read in that context. Responses of the leading authorities regarding the political platform of a party that called "Mormon polygamy and slavery" twin barbarisms, cannot be considered the prevalent feelings one hundred years later.

Many of Jesus's own statements could appear inflammatory when taken out of their cultural and historical setting. Examples are when Jesus is preaching to "resist not evil" (Matt. 5:39), or when Jesus is being led by Satan (Matt. 4:5), or advising others to eat flesh or drink blood (Matt. 26:26-28). If the perfect master's teachings can be made to appear preposterous when taken out of context, how much easier would it be to ridicule his imperfect servants' statements?

Joseph Smith once said: "This morning I visited with a brother and sister from Michigan, who thought that a prophet is always a prophet; but I told them that a prophet was a prophet only when he was acting as such" (*History of the Church,* Vol. 5, p. 265).

Prophets express personal and private views on many topics, including doctrine. These comments, if they are out of harmony with revealed scripture, can be rejected. Certainly, they are not doctrinally binding comments.

30

Are Latter-day Saints Really Christians?

Question: Why do Latter-day Saints continue to claim they are Christians when they are not?

While it is a popular ploy of active opponents of the LDS Church to state otherwise, members of The Church of Jesus Christ of Latter-day Saints are unequivocally Christians.

If we turn to the Bible for information on the term Christian, we find the word is used only three times: in Acts 11:26, Acts 26:28, and 1 Peter 4:16. The only definite information about the origin of the name "Christian" is found in the first of these scriptures. It says the disciples were called Christians for the first time at Antioch. The disciples mentioned were, of course, the followers of Jesus. In its simplest form then, "Christian" is a name reserved for those who are followers of Jesus Christ.

Many Bible scholars agree that the name "Christian" was given to the followers of Christ by those who were perhaps hostile to Christianity: "The name Christian seems to have had its start as a nickname for a very unpopular sect" (*A Dictionary of Christian Theology,* p. 50).

From its earliest beginnings, the Restored Church has been Christian. In giving an outline of the fundamental principles of the Church, Joseph Smith stated:

The fundamental principles of our religion are the testimony of the Apostles and Prophets concerning Jesus Christ, that he died, was buried, and rose on the third day and ascended into heaven; and all other things which pertain to our religion are only appendages to it (*Teachings of the Prophet Joseph Smith*, p. 121).

There is little doubt that statements such as this shaped the thinking of Roger P. Keller, an ordained Presbyterian Minister, when he wrote the following about Joseph Smith:

The fact that he [Joseph Smith] was a deeply spiritual person and a deeply committed Christian comes through undeniably— thus what can a Christian who is not a Mormon say with regard to this religious leader of the nineteenth century?

First, one must recognize that he was a person who claimed Jesus Christ as Lord and Savior. Therefore, we are dealing with a Christian (*Reformed Christians and Mormon Christians: Let's Talk*, p. 13).

In order for critics to claim we are not Christian, they are forced to abandon the simple explanation in Acts 11:26 and use non-Biblical criteria. It appears that evangelicals have attempted to appropriate the term "Christian" for their own exclusive use, and apply to it an unbiblical meaning. One often-heard position states that because Mormons reject the evangelical doctrine of the trinity, they have no claim to being Christian. If this is a requirement of Christianity, then none of the Bible's prophets or apostles were Christian either. The word "trinity" and its accompanying precepts are nowhere found in the Bible, nor can they be found in centuries of writings by early Christian leaders following the deaths of the apostles.

Bible scholars recognize the trinitarian doctrine as a post-New Testament development. The renowned Bible commentator J. R. Dummelow said:

The exact theological definition of the trinity was the result of a long process of development, which was not complete until the fifth century or even later (*The One Volume Bible Commentary*, p. cxii).

Latter-day Saints reject the creedal concept that God is one indivisible substance manifest in three persons. We define the trinity (although we use the biblical term "Godhead") as being the Father, Son, and Holy Ghost, as revealed in scripture. We reject the teachings of men as found in such documents as the Nicene and Athanasian creeds.

To insist that a belief in the creedal trinity is requisite to being Christian is to assert that for 300 years after the New Testament was completed, tens of thousands of Jesus's followers were not really Christian—a foolish notion!

Anyone maintaining that Latter-day Saints are not Christian must also ignore the contents of the Book of Mormon or argue that Latter-day Saints don't believe their own book. From the Book of Mormon we learn that whoever is obedient to the Savior:

> ... shall be found at the right hand of God, for he shall know the name by which he is called; for he shall be called by the name of Christ (Mosiah 5:9).

As Christians, we affirm Nephi's declaration:

> We talk of Christ, we rejoice in Christ, we preach of Christ, we prophesy of Christ, and we write according to our prophecies, that our children may know to what source they may look for a remission of their sins (2 Nephi 25:26).

The Church of Jesus Christ of Latter-day Saints teaches its members to have faith in the Jesus of the New Testament who was not a mere man, but was the Only Begotten, the divine Son of God.

The author proposes that the true test of whether one is Christian or not lies in whether he is trying to conform his beliefs and behaviors to those of the Savior. An examination of Latter-day Saint doctrines, in contrast with other Christian church doctrines, will reveal that Latter-day Saints are indeed in harmony with Christ. We have rejected such doctrines as "original sin," "infant baptism," and the "creedal trinity" as ideas not found in the teachings of Jesus—indeed not found in the New Testament at all.

As to whether our behavior conforms to that of Jesus, the world must judge. But if being Christian means that as a people we acknowledge Jesus as Lord and Savior and that we accept the Bible as God's inspired word to be obeyed and followed, then indeed we qualify for the label of Christian.

31
Why Don't Latter-day Saints Avoid "Endless Genealogy"?

Question: If genealogies are as important as Latter-day Saints say, why does the New Testament tell Christians to avoid endless genealogies (1 Timothy 1:4, Titus 3:9)?

The warning by Paul against genealogy does seem strange—not so much in light of our teachings, but because of the Bible's emphasis on the importance of genealogies and because of the many genealogies of the prophets and of Christ himself recorded in the Old and New Testaments (Matt 1:2-17, Luke 3:23-38).

See what the prophet Nehemiah wrote about genealogy and who put it in his heart to record genealogy. Did God change his mind on the subject?:

> And my God put into mine heart to gather together the nobles, and the rulers, and the people, that they might be reckoned by genealogy. And I found a register of the genealogy of them which came up at the first, and found written therein (Neh. 7:5).

This prophet then takes the next 55 verses to list the people's genealogy.

The genealogy Paul was warning against was not genealogy per se, but the practice of making long lists of ancestors to justify a claim to greatness or righteousness by way of lineage. Many genealogies in his day were heavily embellished with heroic

actions, capitalizing on the doctrinal falsehood that the righteousness of one's ancestors was a type of justification before God.

For example, in Luke 3:8 John the Baptist chastised those who
appealed to their genealogical connection with Abraham as justification for their lack of repentance: "Bring forth therefore fruits worthy of repentance, and begin not to say within yourselves, We have
Abraham to our father: for I say unto you, That God is able of these
stones to raise up children unto Abraham."

Another example is John 8:31-33, where the Lord was trying to
teach a group of Jews that his word would make them free. Those
Jews, themselves followers of Jesus, answered, "We be Abraham's
seed, and were never in bondage to any man." They exhibited the
prevailing attitude, about their being righteous because of their
important ancestors, that prevented other Jews from turning to Jesus
Christ. This is exactly what Paul was warning against in 1 Timothy
1:4 and Titus 3:9. This attitude is nothing like that exhibited by Latter-day Saints in their genealogical efforts today.

Yet as it was in Christ's time with the children of Abraham, so it
is today with some ex-Mormons who often appeal to their Mormon
ancestry or genealogy ("I'm a fifth-generation Mormon!") to give
supposed credibility to their fallacious statements.

The recording of genealogy is not evil or to be avoided, for if it
were, why would genealogical records be included numerous times
in the Bible? God surely would never inspire Nehemiah (Neh. 7:5),
Matthew (Matthew 1:1-16) or Luke (Luke 3:23-38) to do something evil!

32

Is Man Saved By Grace, or Works?

Question: Christians believe they are saved by grace alone. Why do Latter-day Saints think works save them?

The "grace vs. works" controversy has been raging since Martin Luther's time and perhaps since the era of Peter and Paul. Roman Catholics today tend to believe that salvation requires certain works, while the Protestants' most often-quoted scripture is,

By grace are ye saved through faith; and that not of yourselves: it is the gift of God.
Not of works, lest any man should boast (Eph. 2:8-9).

Where do Latter-day Saints fit in? To correctly understand the answer, we must understand how the word "saved" is used by those who believe they are already saved through grace. As many Protestants have explained to the author, salvation to them means they are saved from hell and automatically guaranteed a spot in heaven, based only on their confession of a belief in Jesus Christ. One of their most popular justifications for such a belief is the alleged "conversion" of the thief on the cross. They believe that if they die at any given moment after they have accepted Jesus Christ, they will be guaranteed everlasting life with Christ in heaven.

Latter-day Saints believe that through Christ's atonement and his resurrection, *all* will live again, be resurrected and have immortality. As stated in 1 Cor. 15:22, "For as in Adam all die, even so in

Christ shall all be made alive." Let us look at the question again. Do Latter-Day Saints believe we are saved by grace alone? If being saved means being resurrected and thus having immortality, the answer is yes. Immortality comes entirely through the grace of God and His son, Jesus Christ. Such immortality or "saved" condition is automatically received by all mankind, regardless of how we live or whether we profess a belief in Christ.

However, we also believe what the Lord taught in Matthew 19:16-25. In this scripture we have the account of the rich man asking the Lord what he must do to have eternal life. The Lord responded by listing commandments to obey, then told him to sell all he had and follow the Savior. He did not tell him that he need only confess a belief in the Savior. The Lord plainly taught in the Sermon on the Mount that, "Not every one that saith unto me, Lord, Lord, shall enter the kingdom of heaven; but he that doeth the will of my Father which is in Heaven" (Matt. 7:21, 22). Therefore, in order to enter Heaven, one must obtain the grace of God and also *do* the will of the Father.

The Lord also told Nicodemus (John 3:3-7) two other requirements for salvation: the birth of water (baptism) and of the Spirit (receiving the gift of the Holy Ghost). In Matthew 24:13, the Lord declares that in order to be saved one must also endure to the end. For Latter-day Saints, obtaining salvation is therefore both an event and a process. Most Protestants believe it to be only an event.

If we equate the term "salvation" with the term "eternal life," then we are saved by grace (a gift from God) if we have done God's will, which means being obedient to the laws and ordinances of the Gospel. When the ordinances are changed or dismissed as unnecessary by some of our critics, such as in the case of baptism and bestowal of the Gift of the Holy Ghost, eternal life with the Lord isn't available to such until these ordinances are properly performed, either in person or vicariously. A basic tenet of our faith states, "We believe that through the Atonement [grace] of Christ, all mankind may be saved, by obedience [works] to the laws and ordinances of the gospel."

Perhaps the single best LDS scripture that illustrates our belief in the role of grace as part of the process of being saved is found in 2 Nephi 25:23, where Nephi wrote,

For we labor diligently to write, to persuade our children, and also our brethren, to believe in Christ, and to be reconciled to God; for we know that it is by grace that we are saved, after all we can do.

Latter-day Saints should never leave the atonement of Jesus Christ out of any discussion on how we get to heaven. We don't exalt ourselves. We don't save ourselves. We don't pull ourselves up by our own bootstraps. Even repentance would have no saving power if Christ had not paid for our sins. As King Benjamin, an important Book of Mormon prophet taught, we must "believe that salvation was, and is, and is to come, in and through the atoning blood of Christ, the Lord Omnipotent" (Mosiah 3:18).

However, once we accept Jesus Christ's atonement, we are under obligation to do his will, which is different from doing the dead works of the Mosaic Law that Paul warned about in Ephesians. If we do Christ's will, we will have eternal life in heaven (the Celestial Kingdom) through his grace.

Although most Protestants think that Paul wrote only about being "saved by grace," which he mentions 21 times, he also stressed the importance of good works and deeds over eighty times.

33

Why Did Joseph Smith Describe "Everlasting Burnings" in Heaven?

Question: Joseph Smith taught that Mormons who are saved will dwell with God in "everlasting burnings." Isn't the LDS heaven just as bad as the Catholic's and Protestant's hell?

This kind of criticism offered by the opponents of the Church is an obvious indicator that they are either attempting to twist the scriptures or that they are grossly misinformed about the Bible. As Joseph Smith was speaking at the funeral of a Church member, Elder King Follett, he indicated how comforting it was to the deceased man's family to know that although the earthly tabernacle is laid down and dissolved, they shall rise again to dwell in everlasting burnings in immortal glory, not to sorrow, suffer or die anymore; but they shall be heirs of God and joint heirs with Jesus Christ (*Teachings of the Prophet Joseph Smith,* p. 347).

It would be difficult to find a Bible dictionary or encyclopedia that did not mention the symbol of fire or burnings as being representative of God's presence (see for instance, Luke 24:13-32 concerning hearts burning). Peloubet's *Bible Dictionary* has this to say concerning fire:

> Fire is represented as the symbol of Jehovah's presence and the instrument of his power, in the way either of approval or

destruction Ex. 3:2, 14. There could not be a better symbol for Jehovah than this of fire.

The Bible is replete with examples of this symbol. In Deuteronomy 4:24, God is described as a "consuming fire." Jesus will appear in the midst "of flaming fire" at his Second Coming (2 Thes. 1:8). The Holy Ghost is likewise compared to fire (Matt. 3:11), and even the angels as ministers of God are compared to a burning fire (Ps. 104:4).

Is it any wonder, then, that the prophet Joseph Smith, while speaking of those who will dwell with God, used such an apt scriptural symbol? Those who are critical of Joseph Smith's heavenly description must choose to ignore Biblical scriptures that use the same imagery.

34
No Salvation Outside the LDS Church?

Question: Does Mormonism really teach that there is no salvation outside the LDS Church?

This question takes many forms. Sometimes the individual will ask, "Do I have to be a Mormon to go to heaven?" One person asked Joseph Smith, "Will everyone be damned but Mormons?" His answer was direct: "Yes, and a great portion of them unless they repent, and work righteousness" (*Teachings of the Prophet Joseph Smith*, p. 119). As can be seen from his answer, not all Latter-day Saints are going to be saved—only those who comply with the teachings of the Savior.

Mormonism has long recognized that there is truth to be found in other religions. Joseph Smith declared:

> Have the Presbyterians any truth? Yes. Have the Baptists, Methodists, etc., any truth? Yes. They all have a little truth mixed with error. We should gather all the good and true principles in the world and treasure them up (*Teachings of the Prophet Joseph Smith*, p. 316).

When Latter-day Saints speak of the "Church" being the only true Church, they mean that it is the only religious organization today which is authorized by God to administer the ordinances He deems necessary for salvation. The Church of Jesus Christ of Latter-day Saints is synonymous with "Christ's church," hence the declaration that if one is not a member of Christ's church, there is no salvation.

Even the most militant anti-Mormon Christian agrees that there is no salvation outside of Christ. Since Christ loved the church and gave Himself for it that it should be holy and without blemish (Eph. 5:25-27), the real question is not just where salvation is found, but which is the Church the Savior established and died for?

The point critics seem to be making is, "Wouldn't it be unjust of God to save only those belonging to this small, unpopular church?" But while we declare that salvation is a narrow path, the scope of this work is broad, encompassing all who will ever live on earth. An official statement from the First Presidency regarding the salvation of those who did not belong to Christ's Church, reads in part:

> We also declare that the Gospel of Jesus Christ in our day, provides the only way to a mortal life of happiness and a fullness of joy forever. For those who have not received the gospel, the opportunity will come to them in the life hereafter if not in this life (*Ensign,* Jan. 1988, p. 48).

It may be that there are members of our Church that give the impression they are members of an exclusive religious society. This is not representative of the official position of The Church of Jesus Christ of Latter-day Saints. We soberly testify that the church Jesus established in the meridian of time fell away, and that He has re-established it in preparation for His Second Coming. He commands all mankind to believe in Him and extends membership in His earthly kingdom to all people willing to take upon themselves His name and be baptized by those who have authority from Him. No one will be denied the opportunity to accept Jesus Christ and receive His ordinances through those He has authorized. We invite all to partake of the blessings of salvation and become members of God's earthly kingdom.

35

Are There Three Heavens and No Hell?

Question: The Bible teaches that there is one heaven and one hell. Don't Latter-day Saints teach that there are three heavens and no hell?

Jesus said: "In my Father's house are many mansions: if it were not so, I would have told you. I go to prepare a place for you" (John 14:2). From this scripture we know that there are, in the life hereafter, several places or mansions to inherit. Paul teaches us more on this subject when he tells about being "caught up to the third heaven," where he heard unspeakable words (2 Corinthians 12:2-4). Paul further describes three degrees of glory in 1 Corinthians 15:39-42 and described the various levels of resurrected beings who would inherit them. All of these scriptures are powerful evidence of multiple stations in the hereafter.

When detractors ask us to prove the existence of three heavens (when Paul has already written of a third heaven), they are ignoring this question: if there is a third heaven, isn't there logically a first and second? Our understanding of the three degrees of glory comes from modern revelation (D & C 76), while the Bible simply shows that Paul, too, was familiar with this doctrine. Yet we are asked to prove this doctrine to the critic's satisfaction using only the Bible, but only after they attempt to explain away the verses already cited.

As far as hell is concerned, both the Book of Mormon and the Doctrine and Covenants teach that there is a hell. However, as stated by

John (Rev. 20:13), hell shall deliver up the dead to be judged "according to their works." The hell John the Revelator described, then, is a place where the spirits of those who did wickedness while in mortality reside until the time of the second resurrection at the end of Christ's millennial reign. This resurrection is described in the Bible as the resurrection of the "unjust" (Acts 24:15) and the resurrection of damnation (John 5:29).

John the Revelator also speaks of the "great white throne" judgment, which follows the second resurrection, and then speaks of a "second death" which some will experience at that time (Rev. 20:11-15). Those who inherit the second death and are cast into a post-spirit-world hell following their resurrection are described in the Bible as sons of perdition. Their eternal fate is alluded to in such passages as Dan. 12:2; Lk. 12:5; Jn. 17:12; 1 Tim 6:9; Heb. 10:39; 2 Pet. 3:7; Rev. 2:11; 17:8; 20:6,14; 21:8.

Latter-day Saint scriptures clearly teach of three heavens and define, in general terms, who will inherit each level (D & C 76:50-112; 80:16-21; 131:1-2, etc.) They also explain the spirit-world hell which will exist until the end of the second resurrection (D & C 29:36-45) and the kingdom of no glory into which the sons of perdition will be cast following the second resurrection and the final judgment (D & C 88:24; 76:25-38).

112

36
Doesn't Isaiah Call Our Righteousness "Filthy Rags"?

Question: Don't Latter-day Saints know that the Bible states our righteousness is as filthy rags?

It is true that in Isaiah 64:6, the prophet makes that statement about the righteousness of Israel saying, "We are all as an unclean thing, and all our righteousness are as filthy rags." Let us examine two ideas relative to the meaning of this statement.

First, our righteousness compared to the righteousness of the Lord is as nothing. As Paul put it, "As it is written, there is none righteous, no not one" (Romans 3:10) and he said that "All have sinned, and come short of the glory of God" (Romans 3:23). Second, we become truly righteous not through our own righteousness, but through the power of Christ's righteousness. Therefore, to become more like Christ we must partake of the divine nature of Christ (2 Peter 1:4) and his righteousness. Someone once said, "There is a righteousness of men and a righteousness of God." Surely Isaiah was referring to the righteousness of men, which indeed is as filthy rags.

Yet the Lord repeatedly taught that we cannot obtain his grace without our own righteous effort. Our Savior told us to seek "the kingdom of God, and *his* righteousness; and all things will be added unto [us]" (Matt. 6:33). He told his followers that their righteousness must exceed the righteousness of the Scribes and Pharisees or they wouldn't be able to enter into the Kingdom of Heaven

(Matt. 5:20). In the Sermon on the Mount, the Lord tells us that there are degrees of righteousness and a certain degree (more than that of the Scribes and Pharisees) is necessary to get into heaven. Teachings about righteousness are consistent throughout the New Testament. The Lord even tells us to be perfect, even as our Father in Heaven is perfect (Matt. 5:48).

To be righteous is to be right with God. To be right with God comes by accepting both Christ's grace and by obeying his commandments, following his teachings and doing the will of the Father.

Those who accuse us of trying to "work our way to heaven" almost seem to be teaching that *we should not* do our best to serve our Father in Heaven and follow his Son. If they are indeed teaching this, they are grossly out of harmony with the teachings of Jesus Christ. Many essentially teach that confessing his name and saying "Lord, Lord" will gain them entrance into the Kingdom of Heaven. These are not modern heresies. The Lord, perhaps seeing our day, warned that those who simply confess his name will not enter into the Kingdom of Heaven, but rather "he that doeth the will of my Father which is in heaven" (Matt. 7:21).

Remember, Christ with outstretched arms did not say "Believe in me." What he did say was, "Follow me."

One of the most vivid examples of how the Lord feels about righteousness is found in Matthew 25. Here the Lord divides the people of the nations into two groups: the sheep, or righteous, on his right hand; and the goats, or unrighteous, on his left. Both groups ask why they were assigned that way, and the Lord answers that the division was made as a result of how they treated the less fortunate—the hungry, naked, thirsty, and sick. The sheep (or the righteous as the scripture calls them) cared for the needy; thus they are blessed of "my father, [and] inherit the kingdom prepared for you from the foundation of the world" (Matt. 25:34).

The goats, on the other hand, are cursed "into everlasting fire, prepared for the devil and his angels" (Matt. 25:41). The example is summed up in a way that clearly outlines the value of being righteous and following the example of our Lord and Savior Jesus Christ: "And these [the goats] shall go away into everlasting punishment: but the righteous into life eternal" (Matt. 25:46). Note that the Lord did not make an exception for those who profess a belief in him. A belief in Christ is only of value to those who do the will of the Father.

Peter also recognized the value of righteousness when he said those in every nation who feared God and "worketh righteousness" would be acceptable to God (Acts 10:35). The Apostle Paul (whom detractors seem to quote ten times for every time they quote the Lord) once counseled, "Let not then your good be evil spoken of: For the kingdom of God is not meat and drink; but righteousness, and peace, and joy in the Holy Ghost" (Rom. 14:16-17).

Latter-day Saints everywhere must continue to espouse the fruits of righteous living. We must defend our "good works," yet we should also acknowledge that we are ultimately saved by the grace of Christ after all we can do. We cannot save ourselves nor work our way into heaven—our works would be as dross were it not for the atonement of Jesus Christ and his redeeming grace.

Part 5

Answers to
Questions
About

Jesus Christ
and
God the Father

116

Notes

37
Is God Adam?

Question: Didn't Brigham Young teach that Adam is God?

From a number of sermon reports, diary entries, minutes, letters, articles and statements, it appears that Brigham Young held the view, at least for part of his life, that as God the Son came to earth and went through mortality to redeem mankind, God the Father also went through mortality to become the great progenitor of mankind.

It also appears that Brigham Young taught more than once that God the Father was known in this role as Adam, who came to this earth and brought one of his wives, Eve, with him. Simply stated, he once believed that God the Father became Adam to begin the human family; God the Son became Jesus Christ to redeem the human family.

President Young's first and strongest statement of this idea is found in an April 9, 1852 sermon (*Journal of Discourses* 1:50). In his subsequent comments on the subject, he emphasized that it is "considerable of a mystery," "that should not trouble us at all," and was not "necessary for the people to know" (see JD 4:217; 7:238, 285; 11:43, 268).

Brigham Young's discussions of this subject were rare in comparison to his sermons espousing the traditional concept of God's role. His above theories were probably unknown to most Saints living at that time, as they are to most Latter-day Saints living today.

The greatest interest in this theory came after his death. Most Church authorities contemporary with President Young had little or nothing to say on the subject. The two best-known exceptions were Heber C. Kimball, who mentioned it in several sermons, and Apostle Orson Pratt, who openly voiced his rejection of the concept. Following President Young's death, with the exception of several obscure statements, no Church authority has advocated the idea.

During the last decade of the 19th Century, interest in the subject elicited response from such authorities as Wilford Woodruff, George Q. Cannon and Joseph F. Smith. These men acknowledged that they were personally familiar with President Young's theory but discouraged teaching and speculating upon the subject. The status of the "Adam-God theory" was summed up in 1897 in a private letter outlined by President Wilford Woodruff and written by Apostle Joseph F. Smith:

> President Young no doubt expressed his personal opinion or views upon the subject. What he said was not given as revelation or commandment from the Lord. The doctrine was never submitted to the councils of the Priesthood nor to the Church for approval or ratification, and was never formally or otherwise accepted by the Church. It is therefore in no sense binding upon the Church.
>
> Brigham Young's "bare mention" was without indubitable evidence and authority being given of its truth. Only the scripture, the "accepted word of God," is the Church's standard (Letter to A. Saxey, January 7, 1897, LDS Archives).

During the first quarter of this century, there arose a new generation of Church authorities who had not participated with Brigham Young in the councils of the Church and were therefore not personally familiar with his views. Among these, such men as B. H. Roberts, Charles W. Penrose and Anthon H. Lund began advocating the idea that Brigham Young had been misinterpreted. This has been the position taken by most leaders in this century. However, from the fruits of his research, in the 1980s Elder Bruce R. McConkie acknowledged the existence of Brigham Young's views on Adam, although he did not accept them.

Modern-day prophets have declared that the Adam-God theory is false. In 1976 President Spencer W. Kimball stated the following:

> We warn you against the dissemination of doctrines which are not according to the scriptures and which are alleged to have been taught by some of the General Authorities of past generations. Such for instance is the Adam-God theory. We denounce that theory and hope that everyone will be cautioned against this and other kinds of false doctrine (*Church News,* Oct. 9, 1976).

It is certain that neither Brigham Young nor any of his successors ever considered the Adam-God theory to be an official or unofficial doctrine of the Church. It was never presented in priesthood councils, nor did Brigham Young declare that it was a direct revelation from God. There is also no evidence that general authorities of the Church ever supported actions taken against anyone who disbelieved the Adam-God theory.

Anti-Mormons have generally raised this theory to argue that Brigham Young believed in a different God than the God of the Bible, or even another God than that of current Latter-day Saints. This, however, is at least a partial misunderstanding of the issue.

Brigham Young frequently spoke of his God as the God of Israel, the God of the Bible. His point of difference was not who is God, but rather what God has done. He was simply claiming that God did something which most other Christians and Latter-day Saints believe He did not do.

It has not been uncommon for prophets and writers of sacred scripture to differ in their view of what God has done. It is clear that God has chosen to remain somewhat of a mystery, even to his prophets and apostles, and has not revealed much information concerning his activities prior to the creation of this earth. Paul expressed this in 1 Corinthians 13:9-12. Speaking of himself and other Christians, Paul declared that their gifts of knowledge and inspired messages were only partial, that they were looking to the future for perfect knowledge and the full revelation of God. He further compared their gospel understanding to the dim and imperfect image seen in the poor-grade mirrors produced at that time, but declared that eventually they would see God face to face.

Man's understanding of God then was only partial, but would one day be as complete as God's knowledge of himself (see also Num. 12:6-8). Many statements and incidents within the Bible support Paul's view.

Following are a few of many examples in which Biblical prophets and writers have differed regarding the acts of God.

	Yes	*No*
Did the Lord cause David to number Israel?	2 Sam. 24:1	1 Chr.21:1
Does God justify the ungodly?	Rom. 4:5	Ex. 23:7
		Pro. 17:15
Does God punish children for the sins of their fathers?	Ex. 34:7	Ez. 18:20
	Deu. 5:9	
	Ex. 20:5	
Does God repent or change?	Gen. 6:6	Num. 23:19
	Ex. 32:14	1 Sam. 15:29
	1 Sam. 15:35	Mal. 3:6
	Jer. 26:13	
	Amos 7:1-6	

	The Lord	*Angels*
Did the Lord deliver the Law or did angels?	Ex. 20	Acts 7:53
	Deu. 5	Gal. 3:19
		Heb. 2:2

The issue raised by these passages is not that these prophets and writers believed in different Gods, but rather that they differed regarding their understanding of what God has done. Thus, it is unrealistic to expect all prophets, authors of scripture or all LDS General Authorities to have the same understanding of what God has done.

The fact that Brigham Young believed that God did something which is difficult to harmonize with the beliefs of former or succeeding prophets presents a problem only for those whose expectations for prophets bear little relationship to the Biblical profile of a prophet.

The following is suggested for further reading:

David John Buerger, "The Adam-God Doctrine," *Dialogue 15* (Spring, 1982) pp. 14-58.

Van Hale, *What About the Adam-God Theory* (Sandy, Utah: Mormon Miscellaneous, 1982).

38

Does the "Mormon" God Change?

Question: The God of the Bible doesn't change. How can Latter-day Saints claim to believe in the same God when their God seems to change his mind all the time?

Those asking this question are probably referencing changes such as the abolishment of the practice of plural marriage and the change regarding Negro members holding the priesthood.

It would help if we knew the motivations of those asking the questions. Some who ask questions are like the Pharisees who were more interested in "trapping" Jesus with their questions than they were with finding answers. Others are sincerely interested in the answers.

One first needs to understand that God is the same yesterday, today, and forever (Heb. 13:8). The problem is that people of various faiths attempt to misuse this principle as "proof" for their beliefs, without properly defining what it is about God that remains the same forever, and what, in his eternal nature, continually changes. His love for his children is an example of his unchanging nature. However, his directives to his people vary as their needs change and as they learn "precept upon precept, line upon line" (Isaiah 28:10). In his Church, both anciently as well as currently, there is a combination of policies, practices, regulations, traditions and revealed doctrines. Some of these, those which are today usually printed in handbooks and bulletins, can and do change—but eternal truths do not. Likewise, understanding among Latter-day Saints has changed, as have requirements and some elements of Church administration. However, no eternal principle has ever changed.

Critics don't seem to understand that an unchanging God is unchangeable in such eternal attributes as love, mercy, truth and justice. Also unchangeable is God's commitment to hear the needs and petitions of his children, though these needs change from one dispensation to another. He will alter his directions, commandments and methods of Church administration to best meet the needs of his people, and is unchangeable in his commitment to continually "fine tune" his work on earth. Clearly, he can and does change the administration of church affairs and requirements without altering his stance on eternal principles.

Here are three Biblical parallels to issues such as plural marriage and who holds the priesthood. Each is an example of this type of change:

1. During Old Testament times, God allowed only members of the tribe of Levi to perform priesthood ordinances. Also, in New Testament times, this was changed and those not of the tribe of Levi were allowed to officiate in priesthood ordinances. For example, the Apostles, even though most of them were not of the tribe of Levi, were able to baptize and confer the Holy Ghost. Now, most churches of today who believe in a priesthood believe it is available to all believers. According to these churches, anyone can perform priesthood ordinances—including women in some churches—ordinances that once generally were reserved by God for only men of the tribe of Levi.

2. In early New Testament times when the Lord personally ministered on the earth, his message was only for the House of Israel. He said, "I am not sent but unto the lost sheep of the house of Israel" (Matt. 15:24). He forbade his apostles from going to

the Gentiles (Matt. 10:5-6): "Go not into the way of the Gentiles, and into any city of the Samaritans enter ye not."

But just prior to the Savior's ascension this directive was changed (Matt 28:19). However, the actual implementation of the new directive did not occur until there was a marvelous endowment of power poured out upon the twelve and the Saints on the day of Pentecost, and Peter was commanded by an angel in a vision to take the Gospel to the Gentiles (Acts 10). Of this event Peter said, "Of a truth I perceive that God is no respecter of persons" (Acts 10:34).

3. During Old Testament times God had, as a token of His everlasting covenant, a requirement that every male under the covenant be circumcised (Gen. 17:7-10, Acts 15:1). In New Testament times that was changed. Gentiles were allowed to join the Church without being put under the yoke of circumcision (Acts 15, Gal. 6:15).

Some of the above practices were requirements under the Mosaic Law, which itself was given to the Israelites as a schoolmaster (Gal. 3:24). Christ's abolishment of the law of Moses makes it even more clear that God requires different things of his children in different dispensations and from different peoples. The above examples also illustrate that at times God forbids certain actions that he later requires of his people.

If the anti-Mormon questioner still insists that "his" God doesn't change and "ours" does, here are some further thoughts:

- In the Book of Jonah, God is described by the prophet as changing his mind (Jonah 3:10).
- According to the Bible, God speaks to his people through prophets (Amos 3:7). Why do our detractors say he doesn't do that anymore if he doesn't change?
- Why did God have apostles, prophets, and teachers in his Church (Eph. 4:11) during New Testament times, and indicate through Paul that they will be needed "till we all come to a unity of faith" (Eph. 4:13), and now many faiths say they are no longer needed? Indeed, that is a profound change!

- Why did the Lord love the church he instituted so much that he died for it (Eph. 5:25), but now according to many (including our anti-Mormon detractors), God doesn't care what church one attends so long as one accepts Christ?

The list of "changes" from the practices of the New Testament Church found in the doctrines and practices of today's "orthodox" churches can be extensive. Students of theology should understand that God never changes in attributes or perfection, nor in His work to "bring to pass the immortality and eternal life of man" (Moses 1:39). But while He and His eternal truths remain the same, His earthly kingdom has been in a state of constant change since the days of Adam. Critics would be wise to not criticize God for revealing "precept upon precept, line upon line" as the righteousness and preparation of his flock change.

39

Do the Saints Have a "Different Jesus"?

Question: How can Latter-day Saints expect to be called Christians when they believe in a "different Jesus" than taught in the Bible?

Paul warned about "another Jesus" in 2 Corinthians 11:4. He also told the members in Galatia to watch out for anyone who would preach "another gospel" (Gal. 1:6-9).

Modern detractors are in error when they accuse us of worshiping a Jesus different than the one found in the Bible. Without question, we teach the same Jesus as taught in the Bible. Perhaps there are those who teach a counterfeit Jesus and a counterfeit plan of salvation, but it isn't the Latter-day Saints.

Let us examine what we can learn about the "real" Jesus from the Bible. Jesus Christ created the heavens and the earth (Col. 1:16) under the direction of God the Father (Heb. 1:1-3). Jesus lived with the Father before this earth life and prayed to his Father that he might return and have the same glory with the Father that he had before the world was (John 17:5). Jesus was foreordained from before the foundation of the world to be the Redeemer of the world (1 Peter 1:20). Jesus was and is the first-born in the spirit world (Col. 1:15), the only-begotten son of God in the flesh, and the first individual to be resurrected (Col. 1:15).

Jesus was born of Mary after the Holy Ghost came upon her and she was overshadowed by the power of the Highest (Luke 1:35). He was thus called the Son of God, the Only Begotten Son.

Our Savior prayed to the Father with these words, "Our Father which art in heaven" (Matt. 6:9-13). Earlier at His baptism and later on the Mount of Transfiguration, our Heavenly Father's voice, coming from Heaven, testified that Christ was His Beloved Son (Matt. 3:16-17, Matt. 17:5).

The Jesus of the Bible taught in the temple. The only record we have of our Savior being truly angry and filled with indignation during his mortal life was when the money changers made "his Father's house a house of merchandise" (John 2:14-17).

In the Sermon on the Mount he counseled that we should let our alms be in secret, and promised that our Father which seeth in secret himself shall reward us openly (Matt. 6:4).

Jesus taught that we have to be righteous to enter into the Kingdom of Heaven (Matt. 5:20), so that when He comes again "we shall be like him" (1 John 3:2).

If we want to have eternal life we must "keep the commandments" (Matt. 5:48), be born of the water and the spirit (John 3:5), and endure to the end to be saved (Matt. 24:13).

Jesus established a church and loved it and gave Himself for it (Eph. 5:25). He prayed that we might all be one in the same way as He and His Father are one (John 17:23). While in the Garden of Gethsemane He subordinated His will to the Father's when he prayed, "Father, if thou be willing, remove this cup from me: nevertheless not my will, but thine, be done" (Luke 22:42). It was there that he shed "great drops of blood falling down to the ground" (Luke 22:44).

Later, Jesus, who said His Father "is greater than I" (John 14:28), carried His own cross and died on Calvary for you and me.

Jesus did "nothing of himself, but what he seeth the Father do: for what things soever he doeth, these also doeth the Son likewise," (John 5:19). Jesus did as the Father commanded him to do and say (John 12:49).

He rose from the dead on the third day. He appeared unto upwards of five hundred people (1 Cor. 15:4-8). His resurrected body was a physical body. He ate with his Apostles after he was res-urrected (Luke 24:39-43).

Jesus gave a free gift, even his atonement, to all mankind so that in "Christ all shall be made alive" (1 Cor. 15:22). Through His grace, there will be a resurrection of the just and the unjust, and the books will be opened and every man will be judged "according to their works" (Rev. 20:12, 13).

This Jesus, we as Latter-day Saints believe, is a distinct, separate personage from the Father and was seen standing on the right hand of the Father (Acts 7:55).

Jesus will come again. It will be the same Jesus (Acts 1:11), with his same immortal, resurrected body. "One shall say unto him, What are these wounds in thine hands? Then he shall answer, Those with which I was wounded in the house of my friends" (Zech. 13:6).

Another Jesus? There is no salvation in any other Jesus than the one clearly taught in the above Biblical references. This is the Jesus that we, as Latter-day Saints, believe in. Latter-day Saints agree with Paul in Galatians. If someone teaches a Jesus who saves a sin-ner without his doing the will of his Father which is in heaven (Matt. 7:21), a Jesus who requires no righteousness, no sacrifice, and no baptism for the remission of our sins, a Jesus who is not now a resurrected being possessing a glorious physical, tangible body, a Jesus who does not appear today to men and women, a Jesus who will not send mighty angels to the earth, a Jesus who will not open the heavens for his children today as he did anciently, then truly the preacher of this false Christ should be "accursed."

40
Was Jesus Begotten of the Holy Ghost?

Question: The Bible states that Jesus was begotten by the Holy Ghost, yet Brigham Young stated, "When the Virgin Mary conceived the child Jesus, the Father had begotten him in his own likeness. He was not begotten by the Holy Ghost" (Journal of Discourses, Vol. 1, p. 50). Why the discrepancy?

While one New Testament passage seems to imply that Jesus was begotten of the Holy Ghost (Matt. 1:18-20), dozens of other passages clearly indicate that Jesus is the Son of God the Father, rather than the son of the Holy Ghost. Luke 1:35 clarifies that the Holy Ghost's role was to prepare Mary to receive the power of the "Highest"—God the Father. Note carefully the entire verse: "The Holy Ghost shall come upon thee, and the power of the Highest shall overshadow thee: therefore also that Holy thing which shall be born of thee shall be called the Son of God."

If anti-Mormon critics would take the time to read the entire lecture given by Brigham Young, they would realize that his point is one that they may well agree with. President Young was addressing those who erroneously teach that the Holy Ghost begat the Son, saying this misunderstanding detracts from the Fatherhood of our Heavenly Father. Brigham Young was affirming that God the Father was the Father of Jesus—not the Holy Ghost.

The Bible abounds with scriptures attesting to the fact that Jesus was the Son of God the Father; he was not the son of the Holy Ghost. Thus it was God the Father, not the Holy Spirit, who spoke to Jesus at the time of his baptism, saying, "thou art my beloved Son; in thee I am well pleased" (Lk 3:21-23, Matt. 3:16-17). It was to his Father, God the Father, rather than to the Holy Ghost, that Jesus taught his disciples to pray (Matt. 6:6-18). "We beheld his glory, the glory as of the only begotten of the Father" (John 1:14); "For God so loved the world, that he gave his only begotten Son" (John 3:16; see also John 3:18, 1 John 4:9).

Passages like these demonstrate that Brigham Young was correct: Jesus was the begotten Son of God the Father. It appears that the Holy Spirit, in some miraculous way unknown to mortals, prepared Mary for the conception of God's Son. Rather than being critical of Brigham Young, our antagonists should be pleased that he defended the Biblical position that God the Father, rather than the Holy Ghost, is the father of Jesus.

41

Was Jesus Married?

Question: Is it true that Latter-day Saints believe that Jesus was married while on earth?

While it is correct that several early Church leaders, primarily in the mid-Nineteenth Century, agreed with various non-Mormon Bible scholars that Jesus Christ was married, that belief has never been accepted as official Church doctrine.

Earlier brethren speculated on several topics, including the marital status of Jesus. Detractors take delight in searching out such speculations and trying to pass them off as the official Church position. Be that as it may, the opinion that Jesus was married, though held by several General Authorities, has not been accepted as doctrine, nor is it taught as doctrine by Church leaders today.

The idea that Jesus was married was taught, and still is taught by many others not of our faith, and they present a strong array of evidence in defense of their beliefs. For instance, William E. Phipps, a Presbyterian minister, wrote the book *Was Jesus Married?* He concludes with a resounding "yes" to the question.

Anti-Mormon critics who try to portray the concept that Jesus was married as Church doctrine have little understanding of the canonization process of doctrine within the LDS Church. The procedure was demonstrated with the 1976 and 1978 additions to the Standard Works. They were presented to and sustained by the First Presidency and Council of the Twelve, then sustained by the entire membership of the Church in General Conference.

When anti-Mormon detractors attempt to represent the private views of past or present Latter-day Saints as being the doctrine of the Church, they immediately lose credibility with knowledgeable Church members who understand the Church's definitions of doctrine and recognize the necessity of the canonization process. They recognize that the designation of "doctrine" is not granted simply because of who said something, or where it was said, or in what book it was printed.

Read what President Joseph Fielding Smith explained on the subject:

> It makes no difference what is written or what anyone has said, if what has been said is in conflict with what the Lord has revealed, we can set it aside. My words, and the teachings of any other member of the Church, high or low, if they do not square with the revelations, we need not accept them. Let us have this matter clear. We have accepted the four standard works as the measuring yardsticks, or balances, by which we measure every man's doctrine.

> You cannot accept the books written by the authorities of the Church as standards in doctrine, only in so far as they accord with the revealed word in the standard works.

> Every man who writes is responsible, not the Church, for what he writes. If Joseph Fielding Smith writes something which is out of harmony with the revelations, then every member of the Church is duty bound to reject it. If he writes that which is in perfect harmony with the revealed word of

the Lord, then it should be accepted (*Doctrines of Salvation,* Vol. 3, pp. 203-04).

The standard works, including the Bible, do not clearly indicate whether Jesus Christ was single or married. To take either position is to speculate, and either position is beyond the present doctrine of the Church.

134

42

Is Lucifer the Brother of Jesus?

Question: Don't Latter-day Saints have a different Jesus than Orthodox Christians since they teach that Lucifer is a spirit brother of Jesus?

The above statement is often used by anti-Mormon detractors in an effort to make the LDS Church appear to be a non-Christian sect or cult. But it serves to highlight a significant difference between Bible doctrine and the views of "orthodox Christians." The Bible clearly indicates that God the Father is the father of the spirits of all mankind, and that both Jesus and Lucifer are also among his sons. "Orthodox Christians" do not accept this Biblical doctrine.

In contrast, Latter-day Saints believe Jesus, Lucifer and all mankind have a common Heavenly Father. The Bible clearly teaches that all men and women who have ever lived in heaven and on earth are the spirit offspring of our eternal Heavenly Father. Paul taught, "For we are also his offspring. Forasmuch then as we are the offspring of God, we ought not to think that the Godhead is like unto gold, or silver, or stone, graven by art and man's device" (Acts 17:28, 29).

We see in Luke 3:38 that Adam is a son of God. It is only logical that we, who are descended from him, are members of the same family. The author of Hebrews affirms the brotherhood of all men by stating that we are to be "in subjection unto the Father of spirits" (Heb. 12:9, see Num. 16:22). The book of 1 John gives account of our relationship to the Father: "Beloved, now are we the sons of

God" (1 John 3:2). Paul speaks of "one God and Father of all (Eph. 4:6).

We learn from the book of Job that "there was a day when the sons of God came to present themselves before the Lord, and Satan came also among them" (Job 1:6). Job makes it clear that as one of the Sons of God, Satan was recognized by the Lord in their presence (Job 1:7-12, 2:1-6). He fell from his heavenly abode (Luke 10:18, Rev. 12:7-9, Isa. 14:12-14), but that does not negate that he was once a literal "spirit" offspring or child of God. These scriptures clearly show that all of us are offspring of God, our Heavenly Father—including those children who rebelled and followed Satan.

The critic will point to Colossians 1:16 as a prooftext that Jesus is the creator of all things in Heaven and earth and therefore cannot be Lucifer's brother. Such an erroneous interpretation is in sharp contradiction to the passages cited above and others on the subject. The scriptures are clear as to Jesus' creative role and his obedience to his Father's will, but Paul's point in Colossians is not to assert that God the Father did not have spirit children, but rather to emphasize the preeminence of Jesus as he did the will of the Father (v. 18).

That Jesus had a brother named Lucifer is not a new idea to Christians. Catholic writer Giovanni Papini quotes Lactantius, a Third Century Christian writer, from his apologetic work, *Divinae Institutines* 11.9:

> Before creating the world, God produced a spirit like himself, replete with the virtues of the Father. Later He made another, in whom the mark of divine origin was erased, because this one was besmirched by the poison of jealousy and turned therefore from good to evil. He was jealous of his older brother who, remaining' united with the Father, insured his affection unto himself. This being who from good became bad is called devil by the Greeks.

Papini concludes that, "According to Lactantius, Lucifer would have been nothing less than the brother of the logos, of the word, ie. of the second person of the trinity" (Giovanni Papini, *The Devil*, p. 81).

Lucifer, or Satan of the Old and New Testaments, initially was in heaven but fell and took one third of the Hosts of Heaven with him (Isa. 14:12, Rev. 12:9). His fall from heaven was confirmed by the Savior (Luke 10:18). The Devil and his angels are most anxious to inhabit the bodies of mortals (Lk. 8:26-33; Matt. 9:32). All the Savior did, has done and will do, is the antithesis of Lucifer, but both Jesus and Satan are offspring of God the Father, as are all members of the human family.

43

Is There More Than One God?

Question: Why do Latter-day Saints teach that there are many Gods when the Bible states in Isaiah 44:8: "Is there a God beside me? yea, there is no God: I know not any."

While it is true that Mormonism accepts the Biblical teaching that there are many Gods, it is equally true that it teaches there is but one Godhead which rules and directs the affairs of this earth. It is comprised of God the Father, his son Jesus Christ, and the Holy Ghost.

In that Godhead, as Jesus clearly and repeatedly taught, God the Father hold ultimate power and control of earthly events. Jesus Christ serves as his executive to carry out his instructions and divine will. This relationship was clearly and repeatedly taught by the Savior during his mortal ministry (see Jn. 4:34; 5:17-20, 22-27, 30-36; 6:29, 38-40, 44, 57, 65; 7:16-18, 28-29; 8:16-18, 26-29, 38, 41-42, 54-55; 10:14-18, 25-38; 11:4, 41-42; 12:26-28, 44-50; 13:3, 14:1-21, 26, 28-31; 15:10, 16, 23-27; 16:2-16, 23-24, 27-32; 17:1-26; 20:17, 21, 31). The relationship was succinctly summarized by John the Baptist, who testified that "The Father loveth the Son, and hath given all things into his hand" (Jn. 3:35).

The Latter-day Saints recognize" the role of the Godhead in directing the affairs of man, and give full worship and allegiance to God the Father, whom they regard as their God. Joseph Smith taught,

> Paul says there are Gods many and Lords many. I want to set it forth in a plain and simple mariner; *but to us there is but one God—that is pertaining to us;* . . . I say there are Gods many and Lords many, *but to us only one, and we are to be in subjection to that one,* . . . (*History of the Church,* Vol. 6, p. 474).

With this position clearly defined and established, let us deal with the question of the existence of other Gods. The following extract from the writings of a well-known Mormon apologist summarizes a portion of the Biblical evidence that many Gods exist:

The Bible Teaches of Many Gods

There are dozens of passages in the Bible that teach that there are many Gods. These passages call for discernment to differentiate them from other passages which make reference to the false gods of the pagan religions which existed in Bible times.

References to false gods speak in a derogatory tone, condemning the practice of idolatry and the sexual excesses of the fertility rites often associated with the worship of those false gods. Those passages often called for repentance, for the renunciation of false-god worship, and for the destruction of the groves and other wicked places of abomination and idolatry. The LORD God of Israel had no association with those false and evil gods, and he called for their overthrow and destruction.

In contrast, there are many passages which speak of Gods who dwell in the presence of the LORD God of Israel, who associate with him, and who have his same objectives and characteristics. The LORD of Israel is depicted as associating with them, and as laboring with and among them. This type of passage is often found in instances of high praise and adoration for God, in situations of worship, in instances of extolling the greatness and goodness of God. They assert the supremacy of Jehovah in the Old Testament, and acknowledge and teach the role of the Godhead in the New Testament. The passages cited below are regarded as examples of Bible passages which teach of a plurality of Gods.

Plural References in God's Speech

Consider, for instance, those intriguing passages early in Genesis when one God speaks to another God or Gods, using those intimate words *us* and *our.* In the creation account, "God said, Let *us* make man in *our* image, after *our* likeness. . ." (Gen. 1:26).

The account of the fall of Adam and Eve also contains evidences of more than one God. When the serpent tempted Eve, he told her, "Your eyes shall be opened, and *ye shall be as gods, knowing good and evil*" (Gen. 3:5). Though the serpent attempted to mix falsehood with truth in his comments to Eve, God's statement after the fall confirmed that this portion of the serpent's communication with Eve was correct. After their fall the LORD said, "Behold, the man is become as one of *us,* to know good and evil" (Gen. 3:22).

Again, almost two millennia later, at the time of the tower of Babel, the LORD said, "Let *us* go down, and there confound their language . . ." (Gen. 11:7)

These passages all show that there was more than one God participating in the creation, the fall of Adam and Eve, and the confounding of tongues at the tower of Babel.

The LORD Rules Among Other Gods

There are many passages which extol the LORD as a great God who dwells among other Gods. They portray him as being exalted above them and having power and dominion over them. When Moses and the children of Israel sang praises to the LORD they sang, "Who is like unto thee, O LORD, *among the gods?* who is like thee, glorious in holiness, fearful in praises, doing wonders?" (Ex. 15:11). Moses also spoke of, "The LORD *your God of gods,* and *Lord of lords,* a great god, a mighty, . . ." (Deut. 10:17).

Joshua exclaimed, "The LORD God of gods, the LORD God of gods, he knoweth, . . ." (Josh. 22:22; see 22:5). Solomon, as he built the great temple, wrote: "The house which I build is great: for great is our God above all gods" (2 Chron. 2:5).

The psalmists repeatedly acknowledged that there are many Gods. Asaph wrote, "God standeth in the congregation of the mighty; he judgeth among the gods" (Ps. 82:1; see Is. 14:13: "congregation.") David wrote, "Among the gods there is none like unto thee, O Lord; neither are there any works like unto thy works" (Ps. 86:8). Another psalm says, "The LORD is a great God, and a great King above all gods" (Ps. 95:3). And another says, "I know that the LORD is great, and that our Lord is above all gods" (Ps. 135:5). The next psalm proclaims, "O give thanks unto the God of gods: for his mercy endureth for ever. O give thanks to the Lord of lords: for his mercy endureth forever" (Ps. 136:2). Another psalm of David promises, "I will praise thee with my whole heart: before the gods will I sing praise unto thee. I will worship toward thy holy temple, and praise thy name . . ." (Ps. 138:1-2).

Others Not of Israel Recognized a Plurality of Gods

Even those who were not of the house of Israel knew that there were "gods" who were involved in Israel's well being. The Philistines, for instance, were frightened when the ark of the covenant was brought into the nearby Israelite camp, and wailed, "Woe unto us! who shall deliver us our of the hand of these mighty Gods? these are the Gods that smote the Egyptians with all the plagues in the wilderness" (1 Sam. 4:8).

The Babylonian king, Nebuchadnezzar, was recipient of the greatest prophetic vision ever revealed to one who wasn't an authorized prophet of God. The vision, revealed by "God in heaven" (Dan. 2:28), showed the future fate of empires and the rolling forth of the Lord's great work. Nebuchadnezzar acknowledged to Daniel that "your God is a God of gods, and a Lord of kings, . . ." (Dan. 2:47). He spoke of Daniel as one "in whom is the spirit of the holy gods" and told Daniel "I know that the spirit of the holy gods is in thee" (Dan. 4:8-9, 18). His queen also spoke of Daniel as one "in whom is *the spirit of the holy gods*" and said that he had "wisdom like the wisdom of the gods" (Dan. 5:11). Nebuchadnezzar's son, Belshazzar, also told Daniel, "I hear *the spirit of the gods is in thee*" (Dan. 5:14) and Daniel reminded him that "*the most high God* gave Nebuchadnezzar thy father a kingdom, and majesty, and glory, and honour" (Dan. 5:18).

Comparative and Superlative Evidences

Then there are the many passages that utilize comparatives. Many of them speak of the *most high God* or the *highest* God, which clearly indicates that there are other Gods which hold stature, but of a lesser degree. See, for instance, Gen. 14:18, 19, 20, 22; 2 Sam. 22:14; Ps. 7:17; 18:13; 47:2; 50:14; 57:2; 78:56; 82:6; 83:18; 91:9; 92:1, 8; and Heb. 7:1. Thus the LORD is *Lord of lords* (see Deut. 10:17; Ps. 136:3; 1 Tim. 6:15; Rev. 17:14 and 19:16), and *King of kings* (see 1 Tim. 6:15; Rev. 17:14 and 19:16).

The LORD Requires Respect for Other Gods

Then there are those passages when God himself speaks to Israel, instructing them how they should show respect to other divine beings, even though they are not those whom the people directly worship. When the LORD revealed his laws unto Moses, he commanded, "Thou *shalt not revile the gods,* nor curse the ruler of thy people" (Ex. 22:10). And he also commanded, "In all things that I have said unto you be circumspect: and *make no mention of the name of other gods,* neither let it be heard out of thy mouth" (Ex. 23:13).

Other Gods Identified:
Those Who Receive the Word of God

There are still other passages that define who some of the other Gods are. In a psalm of Asaph we read: "I have said, *Ye are gods;* and all of you are children of the most High" (Ps. 82:6). Jesus quoted this psalm in a confrontation with the Pharisees of his day. They accused him, saying that "Thou, being a man, makest thyself God." Jesus answered them, "Is it not written in your law, I said, *Ye are gods?* And then he identified those who would be gods as those "*unto whom the word of God came*" (John 10:33-38).

Joint-Heirs With Christ

His statement aligns closely with the doctrine of heirship which is clearly proclaimed in the New Testament. Paul taught that "The Spirit itself beareth witness with our spirit, that we are the children of God: And if children, then *heirs; heirs of God* and *joint-heirs with Christ;* if so be that we suffer with him, that we may be also *glorified together*" (Ro. 8:16-17). A central promise of the gospel is that the righteous can be joint-heirs with Christ, whom God the Father "*hath appointed heir of all things*" (Heb. 1:2; Jn. 16:15).

As joint-heirs with Christ, and thus heirs of all things, we can also be a "lord of all" (Gal. 4:1) and realize the full glory of being an "*heir of God through Christ*" (Gal. 1:7; see also Tit. 3:7, Jas. 2:5, and Eph. 3:6). This helps us understand the full intent of Christ's commandment to "be ye therefore perfect, even as your Father which is in heaven is perfect" (Matt. 5:48). It also helps us to grasp the full meaning of Paul's statement that "I press toward the mark for the prize of *the high calling of God* in Christ Jesus" (Phil. 3:14-15; Col. 1:28).

This knowledge of the doctrine of heirship also helps us understand who the Gods will be who are instructed to "*worship him, all ye gods*" (Ps. 97:7) when the Lord comes in glory at the beginning of his millennial reign (see Ps. 97:1-10).

Three Members of the Godhead Govern This Earth

The Bible also contains hundreds of passages which indicate that God the Father, God the Son Jesus Christ, and God the Holy Ghost are all separate, holy, divine beings holding the full status of Godhood. Though separate beings, often seen in or manifested from separate places at the same time (Mt. 3:16-17; Mt. 17:1-5; Jn. 12:28; Acts 7:55-56; Mk. 16:19; etc.), the Bible clearly indicates that they are separate individuals who fulfill separate functions (Jn. 5:17-22, 30-36; 13:3; 14:26-28; 15:26; 16:5-7; Eph.

2:18; etc.). They are united and agree in purpose, functioning for the benefit of those here on earth as a Godhead.

The apostle John speaks of the three members of the Godhead and their combined mission, saying, "There are *three that bear record in heaven, the Father, the Word, and the Holy Ghost:* and these three are one, and there are three that bear witness in earth, the Spirit, and the water, and the blood: and *these three agree in one*" (1 Jn. 5:7-8).

Christ Taught Concerning the Godhead

Jesus Christ revealed to mankind the nature of the Godhead who rules over this earth. As contrasted with the Old Testament, which repeatedly spoke of many Gods, as is illustrated above, the New Testament, as a result of Jesus's teachings, focuses on the three divine beings who govern this earth: God the Father, his Son Jesus Christ, and the Holy Ghost. The Book of John, especially, contains dozens of passages where the Christ explained his relationship to his Father and to the Spirit.

With the new light which Jesus gave to man concerning the Godhead, New Testament witnesses adopted different terminology, repeatedly identifying God the Father as God, and Jesus Christ as Lord, and identifying the three as having direct rule and responsibility for this earth. Thus Paul wrote of "One Lord, one faith, one baptism, One God and Father of all" (Eph. 4:5-6).

Responsibility for this Earth
Delegated to Christ by the Father

The New Testament indicates that God the Father has granted unto Jesus Christ, the LORD, specific and direct responsibility for governing this earth throughout its temporal existence.

Thus Jesus Christ was the executive by whom the Father made this earth (Heb. 1:2; Eph. 3:9). Christ came to the earth in the meridian of time as a mortal being and taught his people. He died on the cross to atone for their sins, broke the bands of death and began the resurrection process, and yet will come at the end of the earth's probationary period to rule and reign during the millennium as King of kings.

It is Christ who is the mediator with the Father (1 Tim. 2:5; Heb. 8:6; 9:15; 12:24). It is Christ whom the Father has set to be over the Church (Eph. 1:22). It is Christ who will judge mankind (John 5:22-23, 27). It is only through belief in Christ that man can attain eternal life (John 3:16). It is only through Christ that man can attain salvation (Jn. 14:6), and it is only through Christ's grace that man can become a God: an heir of God through Christ (Gal. 4:1, 7).

It is this delegation of responsibility for the affairs of this earth that caused Paul to write,

> Wherefore God also hath highly exalted him, and given him a name which is above every name:
>
> That at the name of Jesus every knee should bow, of things in heaven, and things in earth, and things under the earth;
>
> And that every tongue should confess that Jesus Christ is Lord, to the glory of God the Father (Phil. 2:9-11).

Thus, Christ is LORD!! He is the one and only God for this earth in the sense that he is the Father's executor, and the channel through which all eternal blessings flow to mankind.

The key to understanding the scriptures concerning the nature of God, then, is to recognize (1) that there are, can be, and will be many Gods, (2) that God the Father holds ultimate Godship over all mankind here on the earth, and (3) that Jesus Christ is the Father's representative and executive, with full responsibility for this earth and all its inhabitants. This is exactly what Paul explained in his epistle to the Corinthians:

> For though *there be that are called gods, whether in heaven or in earth, (as there be gods many, and lords many,)*
>
> But *to us* there is but *one God,* the Father, *of whom* are all things, and we in him; and *one Lord Jesus Christ, by whom are all things,* and we by him (1 Cor. 8:5-6).[1]

---

1. Duane S. Crowther, adapted from a "manuscript in process."

Now, let's turn to the matter of the Isaiah passage which was the subject of the question. Isaiah 44:8 is only one of several passages in a four-chapter section of Isaiah which emphatically warns against the evils of idolatry. Others include 43:10-12; 44:6; 45:18, 21, 22; and 46:9. Note the heavy emphasis in these chapters on warning Israel of the dangers of idolatry and rebuking the people for their sins:

1. The Lord saved when there was no strange god among them (43:12).
2. The people wearied the Lord with their iniquities (43:22-24).
3. Thy teachers have transgressed against me (43:27-28).
4. They that make a graven image are all vanity (44:9).
5. They have molten a graven image and worshipped it (44:10-17).
6. Wo to him that striveth with his maker (45:9-10).
7. They have no knowledge that set up the graven image, and pray unto a god that cannot save (45:20).
8. Their idols upon beasts are a burden (46:1-2).
9. A goldsmith makes a god, they fall down and worship (46:6-7).

In this context, the LORD asks Israel to compare him to the idols and false gods (46:5). He emphasizes that the false gods have no power, while it is he who created Israel and covenanted with them to be their God and King. Note particularly:

1. The LORD created Israel (43:1, 7, 15; 44:2, 21, 24; 45:7-8, 12, 18).
2. Israel belongs to the LORD (43:1).
3. The LORD will be with Israel (43:2, 5).
4. The LORD is Israel's king (43:15; 44:6).
5. The LORD will provide Israel water and blessings (43:19-20; 44:3-4).
6. The LORD is Israel's savior and redeemer (43:11, 14, 24; 45:15, 21). "
7. The LORD is Israel's God (43:3; 12; 44:6, 8; 45:5; 46:9).
8. The LORD will gather Israel and build Jerusalem (43:5-6; 44:26-28; 45:20; 46:13).

With all the passages speaking of many Gods which have already been cited in this chapter, why do these few passages in Isaiah assert that the LORD is the only God, and that there is only one God?

The Israelite nation is described in the Bible many times as a disobedient son, a son who remains faithful to his father only for short periods of time and then looks for another. Moses, for instance, had left the people of Israel while he went to receive God's will on Mt. Sinai, only to return and find them claiming that the God who had delivered them from Egypt was not Jehovah but an idol—a golden bull calf they had built (Ex. 32:4).

This type of scene was multiplied many times over before and after the Israelites reached the promised land. Is it any wonder that the Lord, through his prophets, instructed Israel that for them there was no other God besides Jehovah? Isaiah 44:8 is not a statement delineating how many Gods exist in the eternities, but a statement telling Israel there is no other God over *them*—no pagan or graven god has power, and only Jehovah can save them.

The monotheistic flavor of the identified verses in these four chapters of Isaiah must be interpreted in the light of the dozens of passages cited above which give clear evidence of a plurality of Gods. Obviously, these four Isaiah chapters were intended as extra-strong statements about the role of Jehovah as Israel's God to combat the pernicious idolatry which had gripped the nation. Taking those few verses alone, outside of the context of the entire Bible, leads to a false understanding of the nature of God.

44
Is the "Mormon Jesus" Unforgiving?

Question: The Biblical Jesus is very forgiving. How can you say you believe in the same Jesus when the Book of Mormon Jesus is responsible for the deaths of uncounted thousands?

The question arises from the Book of Mormon account of the wholesale destruction that took place in the Western Hemisphere at the crucifixion of Christ. Admittedly, it is sometimes difficult to understand why Christ or God allow, and even cause, some people to die. However, let us examine the words one pamphleteer uses to describe the Book of Mormon scene and see if the writer's slant is consistent with the text or whether something has changed:

> The Book of Mormon tells us that those who killed and stoned the prophets and cast them out were spared, while innocent women and children died.

One wonders how anyone could arrive at this conclusion in light of the following passage, in which the Lord tells why he destroyed so many cities:

> And because they did cast them [the prophets] all out, that there were none righteous among them, I did send down fire and destroy them, that their wickedness and abominations might be hid from before my face, that the blood of the prophets and the saints whom I sent among them might not cry unto me from the ground against them.

> And many great destructions have I caused to come upon this
> land, and upon this people, because of their wickedness and their
> abominations.
>
> O all ye that are spared because ye were more righteous than
> they, will ye not now return unto me. . . . (3 Nephi 9:11-13).

In 3 Nephi 9 the Lord wanted the following point to be so clear
that he repeated the wording which follows five times:

> [I have done this] to hide their iniquities and their abomina-
> tions from before my face, that the blood of the prophets and the
> saints shall not come any more unto me against them (3 Nephi
> 9:5).

Destruction of the people is never pretty; however, if the Book
of Mormon's critics will compare this account in the Book of Mormon with the destruction recorded in Joshua, they may see why it
is inconsistent to complain about the "Mormon Jesus" causing
deaths of uncounted thousands.

The prophet Joshua, under direct command of the LORD (who is
Jehovah, who is Jesus) destroyed all the kings, men, women, and
animals in as many as thirty-one cities. Consider the report of
Joshua chapter 6, when the Lord told Joshua, "See, I have given
unto thine hand Jericho":

> Joshua ordered his men to shout and told them that the Lord
> had given them the city! The city and everything in it was to be
> totally destroyed as an offering to the Lord. So the priests blew
> the trumpets. As soon as the men heard it, they gave a loud shout
> and the walls collapsed. With their swords they killed everyone
> in the city, men and women, young and old. They also killed the
> cattle, sheep and donkeys. But Joshua spared the lives of the
> prostitute Rahab and all her relatives. So the Lord was with
> Joshua. (*Good News Bible*)

In Chapter 8, the Lord told Joshua to take all his soldiers and go
up to Ai to do to Ai and its king what they did to Jericho. The whole
population of Ai was killed that day—twelve thousand men and
women. The Israelites kept for themselves the livestock and goods
captured in the city, as the Lord had ordered Joshua.

Then in chapter 10, verse 11, Joshua records that as the Amorites were running from the Israelite army, the Lord made large hailstones fall down on them all the way to Azekah. More were killed by hailstones than by the Israelites.

In chapter 11, the Lord said to Joshua, "Be not afraid of them: for tomorrow about this time will I deliver them up all slain before Israel."

In Joshua 11:20, the text states that the Lord made the enemies of the Israelites determined to fight the Israelites so that they would be condemned to total destruction and all be killed without mercy.

The people destroyed by the Lord knew they were rebelling against God. They refused to repent and killed those who called them to repentance. When a people comes out in open rebellion like this, the most merciful thing God can do is destroy them so they cannot continue to heap wrath upon their own heads.

The Lord did this many times in the Old Testament and once destroyed all but eight of the earth's inhabitants because of wickedness (Gen. 7). Those who do not understand how a merciful God can destroy the wicked do not realize that he would be unmerciful only if he let them knowingly keep sinning.

It should not be forgotten that in the eternal plan, it is God's program that this mortal life is a time of probation and testing. Mortal life is brief in the eternal scheme when a thousand years is as one day with the Lord (2 Pet. 3:8). God's purpose is that death will come upon all mankind so that they can move on to the next stage of their eternal progression. He brings death to all, in accordance with his wisdom, mercy and justice.

45
Is God a Spirit in the Book of Mormon?

Question: If Mormons believe so strongly that God has a body of flesh and bones, why does the Book of Mormon teach that God is a spirit?

Several passages in the Book of Mormon refer to God as a Great Spirit (See Alma chapters 18, 19, and 22). Alma 18 describes an encounter that the prophet Ammon had with the Lamanite King Lamoni who, following the traditions of his fathers, was a believer in a "Great Spirit." Ammon used King Lamoni's own words, "Great Spirit," to help him understand that the being whom the Lamanites believe created the earth was really God (v. 28).

Ammon and other Book of Mormon prophets equated the title "God" with Jesus because Jesus was the ancient God of Israel:

> For if there be no Christ there be no God; and if there be no God we are not, for there could have been no creation. But there is a God, and he is Christ, and he cometh in the fullness of his own time (2 Nephi 11:7).

The Prophet Nephi further expounded:

> And as I spake concerning the convincing of the Jews, that Jesus is the very Christ, it must needs be that the Gentiles be convinced also that Jesus is the Christ, the Eternal God (2 Nephi 26:12).

Critics who suggest that scriptures in Alma indicate an inconsistency in LDS doctrine show that they are unfamiliar with the teachings of the Book of Mormon. A brief glance at the bottom of the pages in alma reveals that the chronology is B.C. Jesus was in spirit form prior to his incarnation, yet had formed the earth and the heavens and was the God of Israel. He did not obtain a physical body until his birth in the meridian of time, decades *after* these Book of Mormon events.

Thus, King Lamoni's references to God as the Great Spirit were not out of harmony with the thinking of Ammon, for to him God was the pre-existent Jesus in spirit form. Ammon knew that Jehovah would one day have a body of flesh and bones, but such a lesson was unnecessary at that time.

The brother of Jared, an earlier Book of Mormon prophet, had the privilege of seeing the pre-existent Christ, who explained to him:

> Behold, this body, which ye now behold, is the body of my spirit; and man have I created after the body of my spirit; and even as I appear unto thee to be in the spirit will I appear unto my people in the flesh (Ether 3:16).

In order for critics to make their point, they must first demonstrate that the God spoken of by Ammon or Aaron in the book of Alma is God the Father instead of Jesus Christ. Because the "great spirit" who created all things was Jehovah, this is not demonstrable. Therefore, to conclude that the Book of Mormon teaches that God the Father has no physical body is to form a conclusion that is not supported by The Book of Mormon.

46

Are Some Sins Unforgivable?

Question: If Latter-day Saints so readily accept Jesus Christ, why do they believe that there are some sins which are not forgiven in this life or in the life to come?

We believe that some sins are not forgiven because that is what both the Bible and latter-day revelation teach us. In Matthew 12:31-32 the Lord states that blasphemy against the Holy Ghost shall not be forgiven unto men: "Whosoever speaketh against the Holy Ghost, it shall not be forgiven him, neither in this world neither in the world to come."

In addition to blasphemy against the Holy Ghost, murder is also a grievous sin, and its penalty is the denial of the gift of eternal life. It is God who gives the gift, and God can say who receives the gift and who does not. The Apostle John wrote, "Ye know that no murderer hath eternal life abiding in him (1 Jn. 3:15)." The Lord made his point even more clear in latter-day revelation: "Thou shall not kill; and he that kills shall not have forgiveness in this world, nor the world to come . . . he that killeth shall die" (D & C 42:18-19). He shall die to things pertaining to eternal life.

In the standard works, the Lord reveals that murderers will have a kingdom, for the Telestial kingdom is reserved for murderers and adulterers, whoremongers, liars, sorcerers, and whosoever loves and makes a lie (Rev. 22:15, D & C 76:103).

In the light of these passages, it is clear that it is not Latter-day Saints who limit the effect of the blood of the Lamb, but Jesus Christ himself.

Non-LDS Christians also limit the atonement of Jesus Christ to only those who confess Christ as their Savior. According to their doctrine, Christ's atonement is of no effect to those who do not accept Jesus Christ as their Savior. Latter-day Saints hold a broader view—they teach that his death and resurrection enable all to be resurrected, the just and the unjust alike (John 5:28-29). That does not mean, however, that all are forgiven and are entitled to entry into the highest of the degrees of glory, the Celestial kingdom.

Part 6

Questions and Answers About

Miscellaneous Items

Notes

47

Was the "Revelation" Received in Response to Pressure?

Question: Didn't the Church claim to have a revelation from God in 1978 allowing the Blacks to get the priesthood just to stem rising social pressure?

Anti-Mormon critics who make this claim reveal a serious lack of knowledge of LDS contemporary history. Social pressure wasn't increasing against the Church—the contrary is true. There was little social pressure upon the Church in the late 1970s regarding this issue, especially when compared with the early 1960s.

Readers may judge for themselves after reviewing the facts. When Latter-day Saint George Romney was a candidate for the United States Presidency, nearly every news magazine carried articles on the then-current policy of the Church regarding the Negroes not holding the priesthood. In 1965, 250 people marched on Church headquarters demanding that the Church make a statement regarding civil rights. Around that same time, newspapers in Arizona, California, and Wyoming reported that sports teams from those states were refusing to compete with BYU teams because of what they alleged were "racist policies" practiced by the Church.

But by July of 1974, nine years later, public controversy regarding Blacks and the priesthood was almost non-existent. Only two small incidents were the subject of significant news media comment during the half decade prior to the Church's receipt of the revelation. A suit was brought against the Church because a policy in a leadership handbook combined the role of senior patrol leader in LDS Scout Troops with the office of the president of the deacon's quorum. This, in effect, would have meant black Scouts participating in LDS troops would not have been able to serve as senior patrol leaders. Realistically, this policy was probably intended to teach the president of the deacon's quorum about leadership, but it was viewed differently by some. The Church made an administrative change in the handbook before the suit went to court.

Two years later, Douglas Wallace was excommunicated from the Church after he "ordained" Larry Lester, a black man. Mr. Wallace's independent act resulted in some immediate publicity; however, the issue soon died out, as did Brother Wallace's church membership.

In June 1978 the First Presidency announced that President Spencer W. Kimball had received a revelation regarding the ordaining of all worthy men to the priesthood.

The above facts show that social pressure was much less in 1978 than in 1965; clearly social pressure had declined significantly.

The 1978 change has been popular with nearly everyone except Anti-Mormon detractors, who incorrectly refer to it as a "revelation of convenience." These are some of the same detractors who previously were insisting that the Church was false because Blacks could not hold the priesthood.

Before leaving the subject, it is appropriate to make a comparison between the practices of the Latter-day Saints and other denominations in their relationships with African-Americans. Throughout the history of the Church, Negroes who were members have been fellowshipped in white congregations and have attended Church services with them. In contrast, African-Americans were not welcome to participate with white congregations in many Protestant churches. They met separately and even formed separate ecclesiastical conventions.

Joseph Smith, in his bid for the presidency of the United States, took a strong stand for freeing the slaves. This was in distinct contrast to the position of other churches, which were pro-slavery.

The past pro-slavery, anti-Negro attitude of such churches is reflected in an event which occurred in June 1995 at the Southern

Baptist Convention. A newspaper article summarized the historical situation as follows:

Baptist ministers view apology with skepticism

Some question motive behind
Southern group's statement on past racism

The Southern Baptist Convention made religious history last month when it apologized to African-Americans for its racist beginnings. But local black Baptist ministers say the public apology is meaningless without significant deeds. And they say they'll be watching.

"In the 1840s, the Southern Baptist Convention was formed because they wanted the right to own slaves. In the 1950s, they stood in opposition to equal rights. The problem most African-Americans have (with this resolution) is when the SBC had an opportunity to stand in favor of equal rights, they didn't," said the Rev. George Glass Jr., pastor of New Pilgrim Baptist Church. "Now when they're presented with certain situations in the future, where will they stand?"

The historic rift in the Baptist Church occurred in the early-to mid-1800s. Fundamentally, the issue was a north vs. south, industrial vs. agrarian one. Slaveholders and slavery were central to the debate.

Southerners, dependent on slave labor for the economic gifts it produced, demanded the right to chattel property. Northerners, with their industrial base, largely opposed slavery as a moral issue. In 1845, the SBC seceded from the American Baptist Association. The southern secession guaranteed slaveholders would continue to serve as missionaries, something the national body wouldn't allow.

At its 150th anniversary meeting June 20-22 in Atlanta, the convention adopted an 18-paragraph resolution repenting past racism. There are 15 million Southern Baptists nationwide, according to Jim Harding, executive director of the Utah-Idaho Southern Baptist Convention.

"This is recognition of something that had long since needed to be said. We're just saying we recognize this," Harding said from his Sandy office. "This is something we can't go back and change, but we can set something right now and do something appropriate."

Harding, who represents 22,000 members in the two-state area, said the national convention has been working on the resolution for at least the past two years.

But the Rev. Glass, whose 160-member congregation is affiliated with the National Baptist Convention—a predominantly black convention of 8.5 million—wonders if the SBC's intentions are entirely pure.

"The question is, is it true repentance or a strategic plan for future growth? you can only evangelize a certain number of whites, then you have to go into other races," the Rev. Glass said. "I think we'll see the answer in the following months."

Undoubtedly, though, the Rev. Glass thinks the SBC's timing for the resolution is good, especially since he's been recently considering the National Baptist Church's inability to provide the ministries and financial support his congregation needs.

"This has been like a bad shadow hanging over them since the 1850s. They must realize many African-Americans will watch the Southern Baptist Convention closely in the months to come," the Rev. Glass said. "Will African-Americans be appointed to positions of leadership and governing boards? If this is true repentance, we should already see (blacks) rising."

Pastor France Davis, of Calvary Baptist Church, agreed with the Rev. Glass on the timing of the SBC resolution and also promised to watch the convention's deeds.

"It certainly is a good-faith effort. The proof will be whether repentance means reconciliation," Pastor Davis said. "Lots of people are trying to make a move toward amending with minorities: the pope for the way (Catholics) dealt with Muslims and atrocities during the Nazi era, Lutherans for their anti-Semitism.

"Five months ago, Pentecostals formed one umbrella organization to bring white and black congregations together, and there's a proposal by Methodists to do the same thing with AME (African Methodist Episcopal), CME (Christian Methodist Episcopal), AMEZ (African Methodist Episcopal Zion) and ME (Methodist Episcopal, predominantly white) churches."

With 1,900 black Southern Baptist churches in the 39,000-congregations-strong Southern Baptist Convention, Pastor Davis says maybe the resolution will help deal with some of the grow-ing hatred in America.

"Maybe it'll help solve some of the festering conflicts. My hope is it'll lead to practical change," said Pastor Davis, whose church is dually aligned with the National Baptist and American Baptist conventions. (Harris, Dion M. [Deseret News staff writer], "Historic Rift: Baptist ministers view apology with skep-ticism." *Deseret News,* July 29, 1995, pp. B1-B2.)

'We . . . unwaveringly denounce racism'

Here are excerpts from the text of the Southern Baptist Con-vention's racial resolution, adopted June 20 in Atlanta:

"Whereas, since its founding in 1845, the Southern Baptist Convention has been an effective instrument of God in missions, evangelism and social ministry; and;

"Whereas, the Scriptures teach that 'Eve is the mother of all living' and that 'God shows no partiality, but in every nation whoever fears him and works righteousness is accepted by him' and that God has 'made from one blood every nation of men to dwell on the face of the earth' and

"Whereas, our relationship to African-Americans has been hindered from the beginning by the role that slavery played in the formation of the Southern Baptist Convention; and

"Whereas, many of our Southern Baptist forebears defended the 'right' to own slaves, and either participated in, supported or acquiesced in the particularly inhumane nature of American slavery; and

"Whereas, in later years Southern Baptists failed, in many cases, to support, and in some cases opposed, legitimate initia-tives to secure the civil rights of African-Americans, and

"Whereas, racism has divided the body of Christ and South-ern" Baptists in particular, and separated us from our African-American brothers and sisters . . .

"Therefore, be it resolved, that we . . . unwaveringly de-nounce racism, in all its forms, as deplorable sin."

48

Does "Mormon" Mean "Gates of Hell"?

Question: Isn't it true that *"Mormon"* in Chinese means *"Gates of Hell?"*

This gross misrepresentation can be heard in *The God Makers* movie and from anti-Mormons parroting the falsehood which it foisted upon them. Robert W. Blair, professor of linguistics at Brigham Young University, is one of several scholars who have answered that charge. He explained that in the Chinese language foreign words are converted into characters which, when read aloud, more or less approximate the sound of the foreign word. In the case of "Mormon," it is represented by two characters that closely approximate the English pronunciation of "Mormon."

The second symbol used for "Mormon" would mean "gate," "door," or "way" in the pure Chinese. Professor Blair said the same symbol would be used to represent the second syllable of the names Simon, Truman, Naumann, Gohrmun, or Siemen. The first syllable of "Mormon" could have been written with either one of two syllables, depending on the emphasis desired for the "R" sound. The two-syllable choice would have placed more of an accent on the R: "Mo(are)Men." Instead, the Church selected a symbol that reflects an "r-less accent" or "Mo-Men" sound.

In selecting a Chinese character to represent the first syllable of Mo-Men, almost any one of about 30 Chinese characters that are read as "Mo" could have been chosen. Let us quote from Professor Blair's research:

> The symbol that was actually selected is the character specifically used to represent a like-sounding syllable in foreign words. When not used to render a meaningless syllable of a foreign word, this character suggests "smoothing something with the hand." (If one were to take this literal rendering seriously, one could explain Mo-Men as meaning "hand-smoothed Gateway," or "way smoothed by hands." Further, interpolation might suggest that it was the bleeding hands of Jesus Christ that smoothed the way to salvation!)
>
> What the crafty enemies of the Restored Church have done is to pervert the facts in such a way that only those knowing Chinese can see their fraud. From the thirty characters which have the reading Mo, they substituted one which means "devil" (and which is not the character used by the Church) and then propagated the lie that in Chinese the word "Mormon" means "Devil's gate," or "Gateway to Hell."

49

Why Don't the Saints Wear Crosses?

Question: If Latter-day Saints are Christians, why don't they have crosses on their churches or wear them as jewelry?

Latter-day Saints are among several Christian groups who do not have the cross as part of their regular service or on their buildings. This doesn't mean that their theology is not Christ-centered—it just isn't cross-centered. Latter-day Saints remember the blood shed for us on Calvary each Sunday as we partake of the Sacrament.

To us, the message of Christ far exceeds the idea that he was tortured and died in one of the most brutal, painful ways known to man—by hanging on a cross for hours. Our central message is that after Christ died on the cross, he was physically resurrected and overcame death, and that he lives today with a resurrected body of flesh and bones. Through his resurrection *all* mankind will be resurrected.

The cross, as a piece of jewelry, has been heavily commercialized. In the Christian merchandising industry it's frequently referred to as "holy hardware." Wearing a cross is simply a custom that has never appealed to Latter-day Saints, who tend towards simplicity in dress and a lack of ostentation. To us the cross is merely the vehicle upon which our Lord and Savior died. If he had been hung, stoned, or stabbed, would his true followers venerate a noose, rock, or knife? We think not.

There is no scriptural evidence that the twelve Apostles or Christ put any emphasis on wearing the cross. Surely, we can't for a minute think that they weren't Christians, can we? Consider Mary, the mother of the son of God, or Mary Magdalene, both of whom witnessed the agony of the one they loved as he died on the cross. They were Christians, yet to them and other Christians and Jews, the cross was a highly distasteful symbol of the crucifixions that took literally thousands of lives. Does any thinking Christian suppose for a moment that Mary would wish to adorn herself with a cross? Yet surely she shouldn't be excluded from the ranks of Christians. When Christ comes again, will he be wearing a cross? We would think not. Would Our Father in Heaven likely have a special place in his heart for the cross, the instrument of torture for his Only Begotten son?

The *cross* is not the mediator between God and man. Christ Jesus is the mediator, our advocate with the Father. Some well-meaning Christians have illustrations that show the gap between man's sinful ways and God bridged by the cross. The symbolism would be more accurate if Christ himself were shown bridging the gap, not the weapon that took his life.

We also do not emphasize the cross in our worship because we teach that a large part of the Atonement of Christ occurred prior to Calvary. When in the Garden of Gethsemane, our Savior bled from every pore as he bore the weight of the sins, grief and pain of all mankind (see Luke 22:44 and D & C 19:18).

A related accusation is that Latter-day Saints worship the Angel Moroni, since his likeness is found on temples and elsewhere. Logic breaks down in that argument, since those making those statements would not say they worship the cross, even though it is used the same way—as a symbol. The statue of Angel Moroni is "heralding" the everlasting gospel to every nation, tongue, and people (Rev. 14:6). Moroni was a man, then an angel, neither of which should be worshiped.

Organizations often seek symbols or logos which differentiate them from similar organizations. Latter-day Saint architecture has long utilized a single spire as a distinctive symbol on its chapels, which are clearly recognizable because of their design. To some Latter-day Saints, this spire represents the glory of Christ's rising from the dead and the hope it brings to all mankind. It also represents man's upward reach toward God. This is a fitting contrast to many other denominational buildings with crosses, which focus on what Latter-day Saints regard as the sorrow and grief of our Saviour's death.

50

Is the Temple Garment Unchristian?

Question: Latter-day Saints wear a special garment they receive in the temple which is seldom removed. Isn't this a non-Christian practice?

The idea of having special clothing that is to be considered sacred and dedicated is not foreign to the Bible, for both the Old and New Testaments contain references to garments of special significance. The Old Testament specifies, "Let thy garments be always white; and let thy head lack no ointment" (Eccl. 9:8). The New Testament declares, "Behold, I come as a thief. Blessed is he that watcheth, and keepeth his garments, lest he walk naked, and they see his shame" (Rev. 16:15).

The garment worn by Latter-day Saints that is given them in the temple is a symbol of covenants, purity and faithfulness to Jesus Christ. It is a reminder that, as Adam and Eve were clothed by the Lord ["unto Adam also and to his wife did the Lord God make coats of skins, and clothed them" (Gen. 3:21)], so we too are clothed as a reminder of our promises to the Lord. It should not be surprising that clothing which represents promises to the Lord should be regarded as holy, especially to those who understand the role of the temple in ancient Israel.

The Lord commanded Moses to instruct Aaron and others in the making and wearing of clothing that was to be regarded as holy. Speaking of Aaron the Lord told Moses, "Bring his sons and put shirts on them; put sashes around their waists and tie caps on their heads" (Exodus 29:8-9, *Good News Bible*). These garments were designated by God and considered sacred (Exodus 28, 39:41).

Elder Boyd K. Packer, a member of the Council of the Twelve Apostles, had some interesting comments about the undergarment received in the Temple. In one address to the non-member faculty and staff of the Navy Chaplain's Training School, he reminded them that as chaplains, they too wear articles of clothing that set them apart from everyone else. He added that their religious clothing meant a great deal to them and that likewise we draw something of the same benefits from our special clothing "as you would draw from your clerical vestments. The difference is that we wear ours under our clothing instead of outside. For we are employed in various occupations in addition to our service in the Church" (*The Holy Temple*, p. 76).

The wearing of the garment, although seen by some non-members as a peculiar practice, is for the devoted Latter-day Saints an activity which symbolizes a life devoted to Christ-centered activity. "He that overcometh, the same shall be clothed in white raiment" (Revelation 3:4-5). Certainly it is a practice for which there are several significant Biblical precedents.

51

Why Was Joseph Smith Jailed?

Question: How can Latter-day Saints belong to a church whose founder spent time in prison?

It is true that Joseph Smith spent time in prison. However, the same could be said of the Savior, for both he and his latter-day prophet spent time in prison.

Jesus Christ was arrested and detained after he was betrayed. False witnesses bore testimony against our Savior and he was accused by the chief priests and elders who were the leaders of the popular church of his day (Matt. 27:12). The governor was ready to release him, but the people demanded that he be killed. He was stripped of his clothes, spit upon, smitten, and crucified on a cross among thieves.

So you see, even the God of Israel spent time in prison—and was convicted and executed for his "crimes." Joseph Smith was also unjustly detained by wicked men, having been imprisoned at Richmond Jail, Liberty Jail, and finally at Carthage Jail, where his life was taken by a mob in June, 1844.

During the nineteenth century swearing out false charges against an individual was a very common form of legal "harassment." From a modern point of view, many of the charges filed against Joseph Smith were so ludicrous and biased as to be almost comical. Often they completely lacked any legal substance. For instance, Joseph was charged with "disturbing the peace" for preaching from the Book of Mormon and for holding a baptismal service. In several instances the constables and other legal officers who served the required summons became staunch supporters of Joseph Smith when they ascertained the truth of the matters in question. In those instances where the matters came to trial, the charges were usually thrown out of court as being without substance, or a ruling was made in favor of Joseph Smith.

Other great men of God who are venerated by all Christians also have been imprisoned. These include Joseph of old, Jeremiah, Daniel, John the Baptist, Peter, Paul, and other apostles. Surely imprisonment for one's belief is not as much of an indictment against the person in prison as it is against those who imprison them in an attempt to thwart the work of God.

52

Is Oliver Granger's Name Forgotten?

Question: Latter-day Saints claim the Lord told Joseph Smith in D & C 117:12 that Oliver Granger's name would be had in sacred remembrance from generation to generation forever and ever. Why don't Mormons know who he is?

Anti-Mormons take great delight in asking unsuspecting Latter-day Saints who Oliver Granger was. Few know the answer. Then the detractors claim, "That proves that this is a false prophecy since Joseph Smith said that all would remember Oliver Granger and no one does."

Let's look a little further into the subject. Oliver Granger was the financial agent for the Church who was asked to settle the affairs of the Church in Kirtland, Ohio, after the Saints left that area. The surest evidence that Oliver Granger is held in sacred remembrance is that his name is included in one of our four most sacred books, the Doctrine and Covenants. This, in itself, fulfills the prophecy. The verse also states that the Lord remembers him. How much more sacred remembrance can one have than being remembered by the Lord? Detractors instead imply that the Doctrine and Covenants says everyone will remember him. That is not what the revelation says. As long as we have the Doctrine and Covenants, Oliver Granger's name will be there, and therefore this declaration is fulfilled.

The Bible student will find an interesting parallel in Matt. 26:13. Here the Savior states that wherever the gospel is preached, the act of the woman anointing him will be as a memorial to her. Last time the gospel was preached, did anyone tell the story about this woman? Not likely. But this doesn't detract from the truthfulness of the statement in the Bible any more than it would have regarding the Doctrine and Covenants, if that had been what D & C 117 had said. Her act was preserved in the Bible, and therefore this prophecy is fulfilled.

Psalms 45:17 contains an additional Old Testament parallel. Here, David writes about a woman: "I will make thy name to be remembered in all generations: therefore shall the people praise thee forever and ever." The problem is, her name is not included in the Bible so that we might remember it forever.

The double standard of expecting the Latter-day Saints to remember Oliver Granger, but not expecting all believers in the Bible to remember to preach about the woman who anointed the Savior, nor the woman about whom David spoke, should be quite evident.

53

Do the Saints Have 4,300 Laws?

Question: How can Latter-day Saints expect to be perfect since they have 4,300 Mormon laws to obey?

Faithful Latter-day Saints can expect ultimately to become perfect because the Lord commanded us to be perfect even as our Father in Heaven is perfect (Matt. 5:48). Moroni, writing to us in our day, told us to be perfected in Christ (Moro. 10:32-33). We know from latter-day scriptures that the Lord doesn't command us to do something without first preparing a way that we can accomplish what we are commanded to do (1 Nephi 3:7).

The Lord once counseled a rich young man who desired to have eternal life, which is to attain perfection (Luke 18:18-25). If he was to be perfect, the Lord instructed, he needed to do certain things. Perfection of individuals comes through the grace of Jesus Christ when coupled with obedience to his will. No Latter-day Saint expects to become perfect by himself; perfection is only possible through Jesus Christ, for salvation can only be attained through his grace.

As to the 4,300 laws—it is unclear where anti-Mormons ever got the mysterious number 4,300 which is referred to in *The God Makers.* That book states:

> The present Mormon "Prophet," President Spencer W. Kimball has written these words: "This progress toward eternal life is a matter of achieving perfection. Living all the commandments [there are over 4,300 in Mormonism] guarantees total

forgiveness of sins and assures one of exaltation through that perfection which comes by complying with the formula the Lord gave us."

Later, on the same page of *The God Makers,* the author writes, "Therefore, not only must the Mormon know every one of the more than 4,300 Mormon laws, but after the resurrection, he must somehow discover the other untold numbers of laws and perfectly obey every one of them" (*The God Makers,* p. 185).

On this page of *The God Makers* is the footnote: "Bernard P. Brockbank, *Commandments and Promises of God* (Deseret Book Co., 1983)." One needs to spend only one minute reading the inside jacket of Elder Brockbank's book to see the irresponsibility of the detractors in presenting the idea that Latter-day Saints have 4,300 laws to obey. Elder Brockbank's book contains 120 topics and personal virtues covered in the Standard Works, whose subjects range from *abiding* to *zeal.* He then cites more than 4,300 *scriptural passages* to support these 120 *topics.*

How even these detractors can stretch 4,300 scriptural references from a relatively obscure book into "4,300 Mormon laws" is so "far out" it boggles the rational mind. Surely, this is evidence of anti-Mormon critics' willingness to go to any length to support a false point. And when it comes to "far out," *The Godmakers* clearly leads the way!

54

Was the Book of Abraham Disproved?

Question: Didn't a member of your church and a professor of Egyptology, Dr. Dee Jay Nelson, prove the Pearl of Great Price is a fraud? Why do you still consider it scripture?

The story of Dee Jay Nelson is a study in blatant fraud. Mr. Nelson made several exaggerated claims about his expertise in Egyptian. Unfortunately for him, most of his public claims themselves have been proven fraudulent. Robert and Rosemary Brown, two LDS members from Arizona, recorded several of Mr. Nelson's lectures and radio interviews. In the first volume of a three-volume work entitled *They Lie in Wait to Deceive,* the Browns presented the following facts about this man's "expertise":

1. He did not have a doctorate in Anthropology, as claimed. He dropped out of high school as a sophomore.

2. He was not a professor of Egyptology as claimed, but a volunteer teacher at Rocky Mountain College, where he taught a non-credit course in the continuing education curriculum.

3. Mr. Nelson did not receive a Ph.D. from the Oriental Institute at the University of Chicago, but did receive a Ph.D. degree for about $195 from a now defunct "diploma mill" which was ordered closed by the attorney general of the state of Washington.

4. He did not receive an M.S. in Egyptology from the University of California, Berkeley. The director of this program could find

no record of a Dee Jay Nelson ever having been enrolled, much less having been a graduate of that institution.

5. Finally, he was not commissioned by N. Eldon Tanner of the First Presidency to translate anything.

What Mr. Nelson did do, according to the Browns, is make ninety five claims about his professional and academic achievements that could not be authenticated. He was a charlatan who was at best an amateur on Egyptology while attempting to be a professional in anti-Mormonism.

Before accepting the conclusions of anti-Mormons, it is wise for Latter-day Saints to first check the credentials and personal claims made by such antagonists. It is unfortunate that some anti-Mormons claim false credentials, so it is only fair that their claims be examined and, if appropriate, be exposed. In the case of claims made by Mr. Nelson and others, Robert and Rosemary Brown have done a valuable service in researching the credentials of such an individual.

Now to address the question of the veracity of the Book of Abraham. On November 27, 1967, the New York Metropolitan Museum of Art presented to the Church eleven recently rediscovered fragments of papyri originally purchased by the Saints of Kirtland in July, 1835 (*History of the Church*, 2:235-36). A twelfth fragment had been in the Church's possession for many years, but the reappearance of those eleven additional papyrus fragments has sparked a controversy which may linger for years to come. The controversy centers around the authenticity of the Book of Abraham and Joseph Smith's ability to translate Egyptian hieroglyphics.

Scholars who examined the eleven rediscovered fragments recognized that they did not correspond to the Book of Abraham, but that they were funerary texts from the Egyptian Book of the Dead. Anti-Mormon detractors immediately asserted that the difference was "proof" that the Book of Abraham was a fraudulent work and that Joseph Smith did not, and could not, translate ancient Egyptian hieroglyphics.

Michael J. Hickenbotham, in his book *Answering Challenging Mormon Questions,* gives a convincing rebuttal to the critics' assertions, as follows:

Soon after the purchase of the original papyri, Joseph Smith stated that he "commenced the translation of some of the characters or hieroglyphics, and . . . found that one of the rolls contained the writings of Abraham, another the writings of Joseph of Egypt" (*History of the Church,* 2:236). In December of that year, he said that "The Record of Abraham and Joseph, found with the mummies, is beautifully written on papyrus, with black, and a small part red, ink or paint, in perfect preservation" (*History of the Church,* 2:348). Hugh Nibley points out that the Book of Breathing text is "entirely different" from the record of Abraham described by Joseph Smith. The Book of Breathing papyri were neither beautifully written nor well preserved and were devoid of rubrics (passages in red). Thus, on each of these three points, the Book of Breathing manuscript conspicuously fails to qualify as the manuscript Joseph described (*Nibley, Judging and Prejudging the Book of Abraham,* p. 6 and *The Message of the Joseph Smith Papyri,* pp. 2-3).

Hugh Nibley further observed that one of the three or more original scrolls was described as long enough that when "unrolled on the floor, [it] extended through two rooms of the Mansion House" (*Dialogue,* vol. 3, no. 2, 1968, p. 101). He also noted that in 1906, Joseph F. Smith remembered 'Uncle Joseph' down on his knees on the floor with Egyptian manuscripts spread out all around him. . . . When one considers that the eleven fragments now in our possession can easily be spread out on the top of a small desk . . . it would seem that what is missing is much more than what we have (*Judging and Prejudging the Book of Abraham,* as reprinted in *They Lie in Wait to Deceive,* p. 243). We should also add that only one of the three Abraham facsimiles were among the rediscovered fragments. This fact alone demonstrates that significant portions of the original scrolls are still lost. The traditional opinion held by LDS scholars has been that the Book of Abraham papyri are among those fragments which are still lost.

An alternate view, which is either expressly stated or hinted at by several LDS writers, is that the text of the Book of Abraham was not actually contained in the papyri purchased by the Saints. This opinion revolves around the meaning of the word "translation" as it was used by Joseph Smith. Kirk Vestal, Arthur Wallace, Eugene Seaich, and James Harris speculate that Joseph did not actually "translate" as we define the term today, but instead produced the text through divine inspiration (*History of The Church*, 4:136-137). The Joseph Smith Translation of the Bible (D & C 76:15; 93:53; 94:10; 124:89; *History of the Church*, 1:211, 215, 219, etc.) illustrates this broader usage of the term "translate." Joseph restored over 120 verses concerning Enoch to Genesis chapter 5 where only 5 verses exist in our modern Bibles (compare Moses chapter 6). He did not claim to translate this missing text from other ancient sources, but restored it by revelation.

These scholars believe that the Egyptian papyri purchased by the Church did not actually contain the text restored by Joseph Smith, but instead contained symbolic references to a more ancient primary document dating from 2500 B.C. (Vestal and Wallace, *The Firm Foundation of Mormonism*, pp. 183-86). Because the three Book of Abraham facsimiles also contained many ancient symbols and allusions to this primary document, Joseph Smith used them to illustrate his Abraham text. All of the authors cited above seem to agree that the facsimiles were not part of the original Abraham text but were more likely included because of the deeper symbolism they contained (Seaich, *Ancient Texts and Mormonism*, p. 106; Nibley, *Judging and Pre-judging the Book of Abraham*, p. 7; Vestal and Wallace, *The Firm Foundation of Mormonism*, pp. 183-86).

What is important is not that the facsimiles and text are only remotely related (because this is apparent from the Book of Abraham text), but that Joseph Smith's explanations attached to the facsimiles are accurate. Vestal and Wallace note that 25 of Joseph Smith 30 facsimile explanations corresponded closely to the interpretation of Egyptologists, while the remaining 5 did not conflict (*Ibid.*, p. 188; see also p. 234 of this text).

That Joseph's translation is so similar to those of Egyptologists is even more remarkable when one considers that neither Joseph Smith nor his associates had any prior knowledge of either Egyptology or Egyptian hieroglyphics.

It appears that after the Book of Abraham was completed, Joseph Smith, W. W. Phelps, and others tried to work out an Egyptian grammar and alphabet. In so doing, they attempted to match up the translated text of the Book of Abraham with the Egyptian characters on the papyri. The idea was apparently to use the Book of Abraham as a type of Rosetta Stone or sure translation (Nibley, *Judging and Prejudging the Book of Abraham,* p. 6; *The Meaning of the Kirtland Egyptian Papers*). The experiment was doomed to failure, but it nonetheless indicated that: (1) they had very little knowledge of ancient Egyptian hieroglyphics, (2) they believed the text to be a true translation of papyri scrolls in their possession, and (3) there was no attempt to deceive others by claiming a knowledge of Egyptian hieroglyphics (see Hugh Nibley, *Judging and Prejudging the Book of Abraham,* p. 5; or Robert and Rose Mary Brown, *They Lie in Wait to Deceive,* pp. 238-40).

Though the above has been used in an attempt to discredit Joseph Smith and the Church, it is clear to those that read the Book of Abraham and study Joseph Smith's explanation of the three facsimiles that this work was inspired. (*Answering Challenging Mormon Questions,* pp. 212-14.)

55
Why Have Secret Oaths and Covenants?

Question: Why do Latter-day Saints have secret oaths and covenants?

While Jesus Christ did very few things in secret, there were times when what occurred was so sacred that he didn't want it discussed openly with others—in at least one case, even with other apostles. This is also true today among the Latter-day Saints concerning the temple.

A Biblical case in point is what occurred on the Mount of Transfiguration (Matt. 17:1-9). There, God the Father's voice was heard testifying that Jesus was His Beloved Son. Moses and Elias also appeared to the three apostles and Jesus on that occasion. Later, Christ admonished Peter, James and John to "tell the vision to no man, until the Son of Man be risen again from the dead" (Matt. 17:9). Clearly, he was telling them that the truths they had been taught in this glorious experience shouldn't be discussed with others.

On other occasions the Lord told his disciples "that they should tell no man that he was Jesus the Christ," (Matt 16:20, Mark 7:36, Luke 9:21). Sometimes, after he performed miraculous healings, Christ required that the event be kept secret. For instance, after healing a leper (Matt. 8:2-4), he said, "see thou tell no man," (Mark 5:43, Mark 7:36). The Lord counseled us in the Sermon on the

Mount to pray and fast in secret, promising that "thy Father, which seeth in secret, shall reward thee openly" (Matt. 6:18).

In John 7:10 we have Christ going somewhere in secret, not openly. He made a clandestine journey from Galilee to Jerusalem to attend the feast of tabernacles. John's account tells us that "when his brethren were gone up, then went he also up unto the feast, not openly, but as it were in secret."

Not all of us are at the same point in our spiritual maturity. That is why Christ said, regarding his parables, that some are ready to know the mysteries of the Kingdom of heaven, but to others "it is not given" (Matt 13:11). The Bible clearly teaches that people need to be prepared for knowledge of greater truth before it is revealed. As the author of Hebrews wrote, some are still babes in Christ and are ready only for milk are not yet ready for meat (Heb. 5:12-14). How are they to receive the "meat"? In sacred places, such as the temple!

Paul, himself, when he was caught up into paradise, heard unspeakable words, which were "not lawful for a man to utter" (2 Cor. 12:4).

Nephi beheld "great things, yea, even too great for man," and he recorded that "I was bidden that I should not write them" (2 Ne. 4:25).

Surely, in God's timetable there is a time that all shall be revealed. But for now our spiritual learning still comes to us line upon line, as we are ready.

When people aren't ready for the more sacred things that God has for them, they are instructed to ponder the things which they have already received before being given more (3 Ne. 17:2, 3).

This was true in Old and New Testament times, in Book of Mormon times, and is still true today. After we read and study the Book of Mormon, then we will have the sealed portion, not before.

Christ reveals his word to one when he is ready—not before. Once revealed, it is no longer secret to the one who has received the new knowledge—only to the one not ready.

The sacred instructions Latter-day Saints receive in their temples are given as a preparation for their entry into the heavenly realms of glory, after their death and resurrection. Brigham Young gave this explanation of the purpose of the covenants which Latter-day Saints make in their holy temples:

Your endowment is, to receive all those ordinances in the house of the Lord, which are necessary for you, after you have departed this life, to enable you to walk back to the presence of the Father, passing the angels who stand as sentinels, being enabled to give them the key words, the signs and tokens, pertaining to the holy Priesthood, and gain your eternal exaltation in spite of earth and hell. (*Journal of Discourses*, Vol. 2, p. 31.)

56
Does the Temple Display Pentagrams?

Question: Doesn't the Salt Lake Temple display satanic pentagrams on its exterior walls?

The Church of Jesus Christ of Latter-day Saints is viewed by some extremists among its critics to be a satanic cult. Those who view the Church in this light think they have discovered pentagrams on the Salt Lake Temple's exterior which they conclude are of the occult, and therefore, satanic in origin.

Pentagrams are, by definition, any five-pointed, star-shaped figure. It is no secret that there are five-pointed stars on the outside walls of the Salt Lake Temple; they are there for all to see and admire. However, only those with a jaundiced eye to Mormonism would declare such symbols to be pagan and occult upon viewing them in person. James E. Talmage gives this description of these star stones:

> There are in the walls several series of stones of emblematical design and significance, such as those representing the earth, moon, sun, and stars, and in addition are cloud stones, and stones bearing inscriptions. . . .
>
> Star-Stones are numerous; each bears in relief the figure of a five-pointed star. On the east center-tower immediately below the battlements are sixteen of these, four on each face, and on each of the east corner towers are twelve such stones, making forty on these towers alone. The Keystones of the doorways and

those of the window arches belong to this class, each bearing a single star.

Star-Stones of another kind appear on the face of the center tower at the west. Here, above the highest window and extending to the base of the battlement course, are seen the seven stars of the northern constellation Ursa Major or Great Bear, otherwise known as the Dipper. The group is so placed that the two stars called Pointers are practically in line with the North Star itself (*The House of the Lord*, pp. 148-50).

Five-sided stars have occasionally been used by Church members in various artistic expressions since the time of Joseph Smith. Some have noted their connection with Church newspapers, Nauvoo legion uniforms, with the concept of deseret, and with the genealogical society of the Church. These stars, for the most part, have been pentagrams only in the sense that they are five-sided stars.

Extremist critics, however, lead unwitting readers to untrue assumptions. They first explain that inverted stars are known as "goat heads" and depict a goat's head within a star that has two points facing up, and then say that the stars on the temple also have two points facing up. What they do not mention is that the five-sided stars can be found placed at various angles, only occasionally having two points up. There are no goat's heads carved on these temple stars. Mormonism is vehemently opposed to anything satanic, and critics' allegations are therefore a distortion of the Church's position.

No one argues that a certain type of pentagram is significant to members of the occult. But to imply that any use of any five-sided star constitutes allegiance to Satan flies in the face of reason. Numerous secular organizations, not least among them the Boy Scouts of America and the U.S. Government, have utilized five-pointed stars as part of their symbolism. Does that make them satanic as well? Are Americans who salute the flag and its fifty pentagrams unwittingly pledging their allegiance to Satan? Of course not.

For most of today's Church members, the stars on the Salt Lake Temple are mainly decorative nuances around the windows and cornices of the temple. That some of them happen to be pointing downward has no significance other than to add variety to the arrangement.

Among today's Church members there are those who interpret the stars as representing light and knowledge. Others see them as referring to the Telestial Kingdom. No other temple is similarly decorated.

In his own time, Jesus also had to contend with those who allege his ministry was inspired and directed by Satan: "But when the Pharisees heard it, they said, This fellow doth not cast out devils, but by Beelzebub the prince of the devils" (Matt. 12:24).

Perhaps Jesus' response to this allegation is applicable for today's critics of his temple:

> Every kingdom divided against itself is brought to desolation; and every city or house divided against itself shall not stand: And if Satan cast out Satan, he is divided against himself; how shall then his kingdom stand? (Matt. 12:25-26)

It is no secret that the LDS Church is opposed to Satan and his plan to enslave mankind. Why then, on the exterior of their temple, would they place symbols promoting this enslavement? The clear answer is that they did not do so. This allegation by extremist anti-Mormon critics is clearly without factual basis, and it typifies their penchant for maliciously attempting to portray the Church in an improper light by making absurd assumptions and comparisons.

These critics would do well to heed the advice of the Savior as he continued addressing his critics: "But I say unto you, that every idle word that men shall speak, they shall give account thereof in the day of judgment" (Matt. 12:36).

57

Are the Temple Rituals Anti-Christian?

Question: Isn't it anti-Christian to have rituals like Latter-day Saints do in their temples?

Rituals, by definition, are acts that are performed repeatedly with an expectation of some type of results. In the case of religion, the results involve God's intervention. For example, in Old Testament times, under the direction of the prophets, the people sacrificed animals in similitude of the sacrifice which Jesus Christ was going to make in their behalf. Rituals regarding the Passover were especially evident. In the time of Christ, doves and other animals were sacrificed by the hundreds of thousands yearly in the temple. Yet today, these same God-introduced actions would seem strange, almost cultic. Nevertheless, they were commanded of God through Moses.

In New Testament times, other rituals were initiated. The Lord's supper, baptisms, and symbolic washing of feet are examples of these rituals.

It is easy for others to label something they do not understand as non-Christian or Satanic. Consider the Muslim tradition of facing Mecca five times a day when one prays: it isn't something Christians do, but it isn't satanic either.

Because non-LDS Christians don't understand the LDS temple and what goes on there, some have relentlessly dreamed up bizarre stories that mark this sacred worship. Lately, a small group of anti-Mormons, while professing great love of Mormons, claim a worship of the devil occurs in the temple, which just isn't true.

The rituals we perform in the temple may seem different to them, but different doesn't make them evil. Picture a non-Christian hearing Jesus speak these words: "He that eateth my flesh, and drinketh my blood, dwelleth in me, and I in him" (John 6:56). Some of Christ's own disciples were so confused about the introduction of this "ritual" they quit following Jesus (John 6:66).

The Old Testament, especially Exodus and Numbers, is replete with temple rituals that today seem strange and very different to us. These are God's words to Moses from the Good News Bible, Exodus 29:4-9:

> Bring Aaron and his sons to the entrance of the Tent of my presence, and have them take a ritual bath. Then dress Aaron in the priestly garments—the shirt, the ephod, the robe that goes over the ephod, the breastpiece, and the belt. Put the turban on him, and tie on it the sacred sign of dedication engrave, dedicated to the Lord, then take the anointing oil, pour it on his head, and anoint him. Bring his sons and put shirts on them; put sashes around their waists and tie caps on their heads . . . They and their descendants are to serve me as priests forever.

Later in the same 29th chapter of Exodus, we read:

> Take the other ram—the ram used for dedication—and tell Aaron and his sons to put their hands on its head. Kill it, and take some of its blood and put it on the lobes of the right ears of Aaron and his sons, and on the thumbs of their right hands and on the big toes of their right feet. Throw the rest of the blood against all four sides of the altar (Exodus 29:19-20).

Obviously these rituals are no longer performed. However, those who believe the Bible to be the word of God accept these rituals as being from God and of God, strange as they sound to us today.

True followers of Jesus Christ during the meridian of time would not have tried to get Peter to talk about what transpired on the Mount of Transfiguration after the Lord had told him and two other apostles not to tell anyone else, as long as the Lord was living. Those rituals which are performed in the temples today consist of making sacred covenants with our Father in Heaven. No one in good taste makes fun of things sacred to another, nor tries to bait them into talking publicly about things they have promised not to divulge.

58

Are Church Publications the Source of Doctrine?

Question: Orson Pratt wrote in The Seer *that Jesus was married. Doesn't that make it church doctrine since* The Seer *was an official publication?*

Whether Jesus was married or not is discussed in another answer chapter (see pp. 131-33). However, the question about whether something published in "an official publication," such as *The Seer,* makes it "official doctrine" deserves a response.

During September of 1852, shortly after the public announcement of the practice of plural marriage among the Saints, Brigham Young appointed Orson Pratt "to write and publish periodicals, pamphlets, books. . . illustrative of the principles and doctrines of the Church" (*Messages of the First Presidency,* Vol. 2, p. 100).

It didn't take Orson Pratt long to give Brigham Young cause for concern over some of his articles in *The Seer.* In April 1855, Brigham Young wrote to the editor of Great Britain's official LDS Church Publication, *The Millennial Star,* and asked him to cease republishing *The Seer* in England. Brigham Young stated that while there were many beautifully written articles in it, there were also "many items of erroneous doctrines" (*Messages of the First Presidency,* Vol. 2, p. 214). For that reason the Saints were cautioned against accepting the magazine.

Orson Pratt continued to publish his personal views in *The Seer,* ideas that had neither the blessing of the brethren nor the sustaining vote of the members. In 1860, Orson Pratt, after being reprimanded, spoke in the Tabernacle and repented of some of the views that he had advanced in *The Seer:*

At that time I expressed those views, I did most sincerely believe that they were in accordance with the word of God. . . But I have since learned from my brethren that some of the doctrines I had advanced in *The Seer,* at Washington, were incorrect. So far as revelation from the heavens is concerned, I have had none in relation to those points of doctrine (*Messages of the First Presidency,* Vol. 2, pp. 218, 219). The First Presidency attached the following statement when Pratt's remarks were printed in the *Deseret News:* "This should be a lasting lesson to the Elders of Israel not to undertake to teach doctrines they do not understand (*Ibid,* p. 233).

In the *Deseret News* in 1865, the First Presidency wrote again against some of the doctrine published by Orson Pratt in *The Seer:*

We consider it our duty, however, and advisable for us to incorporate with this which we have already written, our views upon other doctrines which have been extensively published and widely received as the standard and authoritative doctrines of the Church, but which are unsound. The views we allude to, and which we deem objectionable, have been published by Elder Orson Pratt (*Ibid,* p. 231).

Then in an almost prophetic manner, perhaps seeing the contention some of these quotes would cause in our day, Brigham Young stated:

We do not wish incorrect and unsound doctrines to be handed down to posterity under the sanction of great names, to be received and valued by future generations as authentic and reliable, creating labor and difficulties for our successors to perform and contend with, which we ought not to transmit to them. . . . We know what sanctity there is always attached to the writing of men who have passed away, especially to the writing of an Apostle. . . therefore we feel the necessity of being watchful upon these points (*Ibid,* p. 232).

Only two months after this statement, the First Presidency and the Quorum of Twelve again spoke out against some of the doctrines published in *The Seer* and *The Star,* as well as several other tracts. They "contain doctrines which we cannot sanction, and which we have felt impressed to disown, so that the Saints who now live, and who may live hereafter, may not be misled by our silence, or be left to misinterpret it. Where these objectionable works, or parts of works, are bound in volumes, or otherwise, they should be cut out and destroyed" (*Ibid,* p. 239).

What the presiding brethren said hardly could have been any plainer, yet many detractors quote liberally and hang onto every unsanctioned and speculative word of Orson Pratt and others published in *The Seer,* the *Journal of Discourses,* and other works which have not been accepted as Standard Works of the Church.

It should be plain to all who have read the above quotes that just because an Apostle stated a view or opinion, his idea is in no wise binding on the Church, nor can it be quoted by enemies or friends of the Church as doctrine. There is a canonization process by which latter-day Saints adopt new doctrine and scripture. Items which have not undergone this process are not regarded by Latter-day Saints as doctrine, irregardless of when or where they are published.

59
Do Only Prophets Think For the Church?

Question: Is it true that for members of your church, once the prophet speaks the thinking has been done?

While most members have a strong testimony that the Church President is a prophet, that doesn't mean they should believe that everything he says is spoken in his role as a prophet. Perhaps Joseph Smith said it best: "that a prophet was a prophet only when he was acting as such" (*History of the Church,* vol. 5, p. 265).

"The thinking has been done" philosophy may have been crystallized as a result of a June 1945 Ward Teaching Message that all but our detractors have long since forgotten. They love dredging up little-known statements and trying to establish those ideas as church doctrine or position rather than the exceptions that they are.

Let us read a quote from the message and then see what the President of the Church wrote about that particular Ward Teaching Message, just a few months after it appeared. Obviously the detractors never quote the President's letter since it doesn't support their thesis. Is it too much to hope that once the detractors read this letter from the President of the Church, they would stop quoting the 50-year-old Ward Teaching Message?

First the June 1945 message: "When our leaders speak, the thinking has been done. When they propose a plan—it is God's plan. When they point the way, there is no discussion, it should mark the end of controversy," stated a part of the ward teaching message printed in the *Improvement Era,* June 1945, p. 345.

For the full story, a letter from President George Albert Smith, in response to a query about this particular ward teaching directive, needs to be considered. The message "was not prepared by one of our leaders," he writes. "However, one or more of them inadvertently permitted the paragraph to pass uncensored. By their so doing, not a few members of the Church have been upset in their feelings, and General Authorities have been embarrassed. I am pleased to assure you that you are right in your attitude that the passage quoted does not express the true position of the Church. Even to imply that members of the Church are not to do their own thinking is grossly to misrepresent the true ideal of the Church (President Smith's November 16, 1945, letter to J. Raymond Cope, Ph.D.).

Most other presidents of the Church have shared similar thoughts. Brigham Young, strong authoritative leader that he was, was greatly concerned about blind obedience, or members failing to seek spiritual confirmation regarding the pronouncements of church leaders:

> I am more afraid that this people have so much confidence in their leaders that they will not inquire for themselves of God whether they are led by him. I am fearful they settle down in a state of blind self-security, trusting their eternal destiny in the hands of their leaders with a reckless confidence that in itself would thwart the purposes of God in their salvation, and weaken that influence they could give to their leaders, did they know for themselves, by the revelations of Jesus, that they are led in the right way. Let every man and woman know, by the whispering of the Spirit of God to themselves, whether their leaders are walking in the path the Lord dictates, or not. This has been my exhortation continually (*Journal of Discourses,* Vol. 9, p. 150).

One of the most often-taught concepts in the Church today is found in D & C section 9. Here the Lord teaches us to analyze what we hear, reach a decision, and then pray for confirmation.

In addition to revelations, the prophets also issue advice, make pronouncements, policy, and give personal opinions. In pioneer days, they advised on subjects ranging from how to plant crops to what business ventures one should enter. Theirs was usually sound advice, but there was always room for independent thinking.

Generally, pronouncements from the prophets become doctrine only after they are voted upon by the Church members and canonized. Revelations and admonitions from our church leaders should be pondered, then prayerfully submitted before the Lord by individual members, that they may know for themselves whether the Lord has spoken. Contrary to what anti-Mormon detractors say, when our leaders speak, it is time for thinking to begin, not to end.

As a people we should listen closely to every word the prophets state. Anything less would be pure foolishness. Because God loves us, he has blessed us with prophets through all dispensations. He has not changed. He has also blessed us with great minds and promised us answers to our prayers, after we have done our own careful thinking.

60

Did Church Leaders Have Weaknesses?

Question: How can Latter-day Saints believe the LDS Church is true in view of the weaknesses of the early Church leaders?

LDS critics are fond of revealing examples of character weaknesses occasionally exhibited by our Church leaders. The purpose of their accusations is usually an attempt to discredit the person in order to discredit the message he proclaims. This oft-used ploy is a form of hypocritical judgment that all Christians have been commanded to avoid (Matt. 7:1-5).

As we examine the scriptures, we find that when God has a work to be done, he sometimes chooses individuals whom the world might consider the most unlikely people to perform his tasks, i.e., David the shepherd boy, Matthew the tax collector and Saul (Paul), the persecutor of Christians. The Apostle Paul observed:

> For ye see your calling, brethren, how that not many wise men after the flesh, not many mighty, not many noble, are called:
> But God hath chosen the foolish things of the world to confound the wise; and God hath chosen the weak things of the world to confound the things which are mighty (1 Cor. 1:26-27).

The weaknesses of God's servants are not hidden. It is by divine design that they are preserved for our benefit. For instance,

- *Noah* lay naked in a drunken stupor (Gen. 9:21), and yet Noah is described as "a just man and perfect in his generations" (Gen. 6:9).
- *Moses,* whose violent actions led to the death of an Egyptian (Ex. 2:11-14), and who later would be prohibited by God from entering the promised land, was God's choice as the redeemer of Israel.
- *Jonah,* who fled from God's presence (Jonah 1:3), was nevertheless the man whom God chose to deliver his message to Nineveh.
- *Peter's* pitiful denials of the Master (Luke 22:54-62) didn't prevent him from becoming the leader of the fledgling church.

God's latter-day choice of servants compares favorably with his early day selection. Those who would point to a man's weakness to discredit his message or calling have either not read the Bible or have chosen to ignore what they have read. Let he who is "without sin" be the first to condemn God's servants for being imperfect. In doing so, these critics may wish to remember that "with what judgment ye judge, ye shall be judged" (Matt. 7:2).

Anti-Mormon detractors would do well to recall, also, that during the past several decades numerous nationally known televangelists, preachers, priests, and other church officials from among the ranks of "orthodox Christianity" have been publicly exposed, defrocked, removed from office, and in some instances sent to jail by civil authorities. Does their unseemly behavior automatically make their churches false?

In the light of Paul's profound observation that "all have sinned, and come short of the glory of God" (Rom 3:23) all denominations are compelled to recognize that neither their members nor their leaders are completely blameless individuals—God does his work through imperfect people.

61

Why Use Water For the Sacrament?

Question: Why do Latter-day Saints use water instead of wine for communion?

The Bible doesn't designate specific emblems for the sacrament. The Lord, as recorded in John 6:54, said, "Whoso eateth my flesh, and drinketh my blood, hath eternal life, and I will raise him up at the last day."

Matthew, on the other hand, records only that the Lord "took the cup," adding that the Lord said he would not "drink henceforth of this fruit of the vine, until that day when I drink it new with you in my Father's kingdom" (Matt. 26:29). Perhaps that is why the Lord refused the wine and myrrh the guard offered him while he hung on the cross. Both the New Testament arid the Doctrine and Covenants tell of a time when the Savior will sit down with prophets of Bible and Book of Mormon times to partake of the fruit of the vine together in Our Father's Kingdom (Matt. 26:29; D & C 27:5). Only Moroni, writing for the benefit of the Lamanites, refers to wine in the sacramental prayer (Moroni 5:2).

For the first four months following the Restored Church's organization, wine was used as the emblem to remember the blood Christ shed. Then, early in August 1830, while Joseph Smith was on his way to purchase some wine for the Sacrament, he received what became the 27th section of the Doctrine and Covenants. In that revelation, the heavenly messenger warned him of the danger of purchasing sacramental wine from enemies of the Saints. He told him that

> it mattereth not what ye shall eat or what ye shall drink when ye partake of the sacrament, if it so be that ye do it with an eye single to my glory . . .
>
> Wherefore, a commandment I give unto you, that you shall not purchase wine neither strong drink of your enemies;
>
> Wherefore, you shall partake of none except it is made new among you (D & C 27:2-4).

Although new wine of the Church's own making was used, even in Utah for a time, water is now used throughout most of the Church.

Detractors may be surprised to know that many other Christians beside Latter-day Saints have chosen to not use wine for communion or the sacrament. Grape juice is used by most Baptists and Disciples of Christ congregations. United Methodists used grape juice for their communion for most of this century, a custom said to have been started by the founder of the Welch's grape juice enterprise who was a strong Methodist.

As the Lord said so plainly in 1830, it really doesn't matter what is used for the emblems, as long as they are taken with an eye single to the glory of the Lord.

Bibliography

Anderson, Richard Lloyd. *Investigating the Book of Mormon Witnesses.* Salt Lake City: Deseret Book, 1981.

Anderson, Richard Lloyd. *Understanding Paul.* Salt Lake City: Deseret Book, 1983.

Angeles, Peter Adam. *Dictionary of Christian Theology.* San Francisco: Harper & Row, 1985.

Arrington, Leonard J. and Davis Bitten. *The Mormon Experience: A History of the Latter-day Saints.* New York: Vintage Books, 1979.

Backman, Milton V. Jr. *Joseph Smith's First Vision.* Salt Lake City: Bookcraft. 1971.

Barclay, William. *Introducing the Bible.* Nashville: Abingdon, 1972.

Book of Mormon. Salt Lake City: The Church of Jesus Christ of Latter-day Saints, 1981.

Brockbank, Bernard P. *Commandments and Promises of God.* Salt Lake City: Deseret Book Company, 1983.

Brown, Robert L. and Rosemary Brown. *They Lie in Wait to Deceive: A Study of Anti-Mormon Deception.* 3 vols. Mesa: Brownworth Publishing Company, 1985-1986.

Bruce, F. F. *Paul; Apostle of the Heart Set Free.* Grand Rapids: Eerdmans, 1977.

Bush, Lester E. Jr. "The Spaulding Theory, Then and Now" (reprint). Sandy: Mormon Miscellaneous, 1984.

Clark, James R. (comp.). *Messages of the First Presidency.* 6 vols. Salt Lake City: Bookcraft, 1965.

Crowther, Duane S. *The Prophecies of Joseph Smith.* Bountiful: Horizon Publishers, 1963.

Decker, Ed. *The God Makers.* Eugene: Harvest House, 1984.

Doctrine and Covenants. Salt Lake City: The Church of Jesus Christ of Latter-day Saints, 1981.

Dummelow, J.R. *A Commentary on the Holy Bible: Complete in One Volume.* New York: Macmillan, 1936.

Enns, Paul P. *The Moody Handbook of Theology.* Chicago: Moody Press, 1989.

Ensign. Salt Lake City: The Church of Jesus Christ of Latter-day Saints.

Evenson, Darrick T. *The Gainsayers.* Bountiful: Horizon Publishers, 1989.

Forrest, Bill. "Are Mormons Christian?" Sandy: Mormon Miscellaneous, n.d.

Forrest, Bill and Van Hale. "Scrapbook of Mormon Polemics", #1 and #2. Sandy: Mormon Miscellaneous, 1986.

Good News Bible. Glasgow: Collins/Fontana, 1979.

Goetzmann, William N. *The Case of the Missing Phylactery.* Worcester: American Antiquarian Society, 1985.

Griffith, Michael T. *Refuting the Critics.* Bountiful: Horizon Publishers, 1993.

Hale, Van. "Defining the Mormon Doctrine of Deity". Reprint #6. Sandy: Mormon Miscellaneous, 1982

Hale, Van. "How Could a Prophet Believe in Moonmen?" Sandy: Mormon Miscellaneous, 1983.

Hale, Van. "What About the Adam-God Theory?" Response #3. Sandy: Mormon Miscellaneous, 1982.

Harrison, G. T. *Mormons Are Peculiar People.* New York: Vantage Press, 1954.

Journal of Discourses, 8th reprint. Salt lake City: Deseret Book, 1974.

Keller, Roger R. *Reformed Christians and Mormon Christians: Lets Talk.* United States: Pryor Pettingill, 1986.

Kimball, Edward L. (ed). *The Teaching of Spencer W Kimball.* Salt Lake City: Bookcraft, 1982.

Larson, Stan. "Changes in the Early Texts of the Book of Mormon" (reprint). Provo: Foundation for Ancient Research and Book of Mormon Studies (FARMS), 1976.

Larson, Stan. "Textual Variants in Book of Mormon Manuscripts" (reprint). Provo: FARMS, 1977.

LDS Bible Dictionary in the *Holy Bible.* Salt Lake City: The Church of Jesus Christ of Latter-day Saints, 1979.

LDS Missionary Bible Ready References in the *Holy Bible.* Cambridge, Great Britain: Cambridge University Press, 1950.

LDS Topical Guide to the Scriptures. Salt Lake City: The Church of Jesus Christ of Latter-day Saints, 1977.

Ludlow, Daniel H. *A Companion to Your Study of the Book of Mormon.* Salt Lake City: Deseret Book, 1976.

McConkie, Bruce R. *A New Witness for the Articles of Faith.* Salt Lake City: Deseret Book, 1985.

McConkie, Bruce R. *Doctrinal New Testament Commentary.* 3 vols. Salt Lake City: Bookcraft, 1987.

McConkie, Bruce R. (comp.). *Doctrines of Salvation.* 3 vols. Salt Lake City: Bookcraft, 1989.

McConkie, Bruce R. *Mormon Doctrine.* 2nd Edition. Salt Lake City: Bookcraft, 1966.

McConkie, Joseph Fielding and Robert Millet. *Sustaining and Defending the Faith.* Salt Lake City: Bookcraft, 1985.

Metzger, Bruce Manning. *Text of the New Testament—Its Transmission, Corruption and Restoration.* United States: Rheims, 1964.

Millet, Robert L. *By Grace Are We Saved.* Salt Lake City: Bookcraft, 1989.

Millet, Robert L. *To Be Learned Is Good If.* Salt Lake City: Bookcraft, 1987.

Nibley, Hugh. "Judging and Prejudging the Book of Abraham" (reprint). Provo: FARMS, 1979.

Nibley, Hugh. "The Meaning of the Kirtland Egyptian Papers" (reprint). Provo: FARMS, 1972.

Nibley, Hugh. *Myth Makers.* Salt Lake City: Bookcraft, 1961.

Nibley, Hugh. *Since Cumorah.* Salt Lake City: Deseret Book, 1967.

Packer, Boyd K. *The Holy Temple.* Salt Lake City: Bookcraft, 1980.

Papini, Giovanni. *The Devil;* translated from *The Italian,* by Adrienne Foulke. New York: Dutton, 1954.

Pearl of Great Price. Salt Lake City: The Church of Jesus Christ of Latter-day Saints, 1981.

Peloubet, F. N. *Peloubet's Bible Dictionary.* Philadelphia: The J. C. Winston Company, 1925.

Peterson, Daniel C. and Stephen Ricks. *Offenders for a Word.* Salt Lake City: Aspen Books, 1992.

Phipps, William E. *Was Jesus Married? The Distortion of Sexuality in the Christian Tradition.* New York: Harper & Row, 1970.

Pratt, Orson. *The Seer.* Salt lake City: Seagull Book & Tape, 1993.

"Response to Mormonism—Shadow or Reality?" Response #6. Sandy: Mormon Miscellaneous, 1983.

Richardson, Alan. *A Dictionary of Christian Theology.* Philadelphia: Westminster Press, 1969.

Robinson, Steven E. *Are Mormons Christians?* Salt lake City: Bookcraft, 1991.

Scharffs, Gilbert W. *The Truth About the Godmakers.* Salt lake City: Publishers Press, 1986.

Seaich, Eugene. *Ancient Texts and Mormonism.* Murray: Sounds of Zion, 1983.

Smith, Joseph Jr. *History of the Church.* 7 vols. Salt Lake City: Deseret Book, 1978.

Smith, Joseph Fielding. *Doctrines of Salvation.* 3 vols. Salt Lake City: Bookcraft, 1954-1956.

Smith, Joseph Fielding (comp.). *Teachings of the Prophet Joseph Smith.* Salt Lake City: Deseret Book, 1977.

Smith, Joseph Fielding, Jr. *Answers to Gospel Questions.* 6 vols. Salt lake City: Deseret Book, 1960.

Sorenson, John L. "An Evaluation of the Smithsonian Institute–Statement Regarding the Book of Mormon" (reprint). Provo: FARMS, 1991.

A Sure Foundation: Answers to Difficult Gospel Questions. Salt Lake City: Deseret Book, 1988.

Talmage, James E. *The House of the Lord; A Study of Holy Sanctuaries, Ancient and Modern.* Salt Lake City: Bookcraft, 1962.

Vestal, Kirk H. and Arthur Wallace. *The Firm Foundation of Mormonism.* Los Angeles: LL Company, 1981.

View of the Hebrews: An Unparallel. Provo: FARMS, 1983.

Wells, Robert E. *We Are Christians Because . , ,* Salt Lake City: Deseret Book, 1985.

"What The Mormons Think of Christ". Salt Lake City: The Church of Jesus Christ of Latter-day Saints.

Wood, Wilford C. *Joseph Smith Begins His Work.* Salt Lake City: Wilford C. Wood, 1962.

Index

A

Adam-God Theory, 118-19
Angelic Visitations, 50-52, 74
Anti-Mormon Tactics and Arguments
  Characteristics of 29, 38, 161,172-73
  Portray Mormons as Anti-Bible, 55
  Put unorthodox spins on words, 76
  Claim Mormon ancestry, 102
  Assume statements by Church leaders doctrine, 94-96
Athanasian Creed, 99
Articles of Faith,
  Quotations from, 18, 55, 60, 104
Armana letters, 19

B

Barclay, William,
  British Bible expositor, 45
Blair, Robert W., Professor of linguistics, statement by, 161-62
Bible
  Quotations from, 15, 25-28, 33, 49-54, 58-59, 66, 67, 70-71,
  74-75, 83, 86, 89, 92-93, 101-04, 107, 110-14, 122-30, 134-46,
  149, 152-53, 164, 166-68, 171, 172-73, 179-80, 184, 186,
  195-96, 120
  Translation of, 60-61
Book of Mormon
  Quotations from, 16, 19, 22, 24, 33, 35, 72, 90-91, 99, 105,
  148-51, 172-73, 180, 196
  Printing of, 42-45
Brown, Robert and Rosemary, 174-75
Bruce, F. F., statement by, 54

M

T

V

W

Y